THE
CANUCKS

Library and Archives Canada Cataloguing in Publication data available upon request.

We acknowledge the financial support of the Government of Canada through the Book Publishing Industry Development Program and that of the Government of Ontario through the Ontario Media Development Corporation's Ontario Book Initiative. We further acknowledge the support of the Canada Council for the Arts and the Ontario Arts Council for our publishing program.

Designed by First Image
Printed and bound in the United States of America

All photographs copyright NHL/Getty Images

FENN / McClelland & Stewart Ltd.
75 Sherbourne Street
Toronto, Ontario
M5A 2P9
www.mcclelland.com

Celebrating the 2010–2011 Season
of the
VANCOUVER CANUCKS

OFFICIAL LICENSED PRODUCT
NHL
PRODUIT LICENCIE OFFICIEL

Andrew Podnieks

FENN

M&S

CONTENTS

Conference Final
Vancouver vs. San Jose

Vancouver wins best-of-seven 4-1

Stanley Cup Final

Boston wins best-of-seven 4-3

Team History

INTRODUCTION

In the end, the Vancouver Canucks were one win shy of a perfect season.

It's one thing to start the year as a Stanley Cup favourite, and another thing altogether to get to game seven of the Stanley Cup Final after many exhibition games, eighty-two games in the regular season, and four grueling rounds of the playoffs. But the Vancouver Canucks did almost make it in 2010-11. Unfortunately, they fell just short, losing on home ice to Boston, 4–0, in the final and decisive game of the season.

Most of the elements for a long season seemed in place at the start of the year. Goalie Roberto Luongo had been a mainstay in the crease for several years now and proved he could win at the highest level when he backstopped Canada to Olympic gold in February 2010. The Sedin twins—Daniel the scorer and Henrik, the captain and passer—were at the height of their powers, leaders and stars of the offense.

Ryan Kesler emerged in 2010-11 as a dominant player, a power forward who could score, pass, and, remarkably, play shutdown defence. And speaking of defence, the Canucks had a tremendous corps of blue-liners, beginning with the persevering Sami Salo and including Dan Hamhuis and Christian Ehrhoff.

Putting all the pieces together was coach Alain Vigneault, and above him was general manager Mike Gillis, who was nothing short of masterful. In all, he signed nine free agents in the summer of 2010, and during the season he made several trades to acquire key pieces to the puzzle, including Chris Higgins, Maxim Lapierre, and Victor Oreskovich.

Perhaps most notably, the team's scouting deserves credit. The team had twelve of its own draft choices in the lineup during the season, but only three—the Sedins and Kesler—were selected in the first round. Many were late selections, clearly indicating the value of the scouting department to the team's success.

And then came the playoffs. The Canucks finished first overall in the league, giving them home-ice advantage throughout the post-season, an advantage they needed and used appropriately at several key moments. The first such game came in the opening round when the Chicago Blackhawks rallied from 3–0 down to force a game seven, but home ice helped carry the Canucks to a 2–1 win in overtime and demystify a team that had eliminated them the previous two years.

In the second round, the team was led by Luongo and Kesler, and in the third round Kesler scored a huge goal—perhaps the most important of the playoffs—late in game five against San Jose. The goal tied the game, 2–2, and the Canucks won in overtime, winning in five games and giving them a week's rest. A loss might well have been their undoing.

And then the Stanley Cup Final, a showcase they have participated in only twice before, losing both times. It was a strange series through six games, as the Canucks won three close decisions at home and suffered three bad losses in Boston. These results merely set the stage for a dramatic game seven at Rogers Arena, winner take all, but it was the Bruins who had that extra bit of energy and won the Cup.

Nevertheless, a season that began nearly ten months ago with thirty teams fighting for the Stanley Cup came down to one game, and the Canucks were in that game. Great season. Not the desired ending, but 2010-11 was a wild ride all the same.

Canucks players celebrate their overtime win in game five against San Jose to advance to the Stanley Cup Final.

THE BIRTH OF THE VANCOUVER CANUCKS

The first professional hockey team in Vancouver was established by Lester and Frank Patrick in 1911 as part of the Pacific Coast Hockey League, a western league that hoped to challenge the dominant National Hockey Association in the East, which centred around the Toronto-Ottawa-Montreal corridor.

And so was born the Vancouver Millionaires who played out of the new Denman Arena. The team won the Stanley Cup in 1915, the first time a team so far west had ever won. Frank Patrick was the coach, and the lineup featured several well-known players including Cyclone Taylor, Hugh Lehman, and Frank Nighbor. They beat the Ottawa Senators in three straight games by scores of 6–2, 8–3, and 12–3. The Millionaires survived until 1926, after which Vancouver had only minor hockey for nearly two decades.

But in 1945, the Pacific Coast Hockey League added Vancouver to its league. The team selected a nickname based on Johnny Canuck, a cartoon character created for political satire in 1869. Johnny Canuck re-emerged during the Second World War, making him a well-known and current character when Vancouver joined the PCHL.

The team had immediate success, winning the league championship in its first season and again in 1947–48. In 1952, the PCHL merged with the Western Canada Senior Hockey League to form the Western Hockey League, and the Canucks continued their winning ways, capturing league titles in 1958, 1960, 1969, and 1970. The WHL team folded as soon as the city got its NHL team, that summer.

In 1965 the NHL announced its intentions to expand from six teams to twelve by 1967, and Canucks owner Fred Hume put together a bid towards this ambition. Although the bid failed, the Pacific Coliseum was nonetheless built in 1967, with the NHL in mind. It was a fortuitous gamble, for the city got a franchise in 1970, along with Buffalo.

The team played its first regular-season game on October 9, 1970, losing 3–1 to Los Angeles. The team's only goal—and the first in franchise history—was scored by Barry Wilkins. Two days later, the Canucks won their first game, a 5–3 decision over Toronto.

The team played out of the Pacific Coliseum from 1970 until 1995, at which time a new and modern facility was opened. It was first known as General Motors (GM) Place, but a sponsorship change brought a new name starting with the 2010–11 season, after which it has been called Rogers Arena.

Cesare Maniago.

ROGERS ARENA AND PACIFIC COLISEUM

Although it has faded in the mind's eye because of the prominence of Rogers Arena on the hockey landscape, the Pacific Coliseum holds an important place in hockey history, in British Columbia, and for all of Canada. Built in 1966–67, it opened in 1968 and was the home rink for the Vancouver Canucks of the WHL for two years. It also hosted the first Canucks game when the franchise joined the NHL in 1970.

In the early days its most famous moment came on September 8, 1972, when Canada and the Soviet Union played game four of the Summit Series there. After teams won, lost, and tied a game in the first three games in Montreal, Toronto, and Winnipeg, the final game in Canada was pivotal. But CCCP won that game, 5–3, and fans booed Team Canada off the ice, leading to Phil Esposito's famous "we're trying our best" speech with Johnny Esaw at ice level right after.

General Motors (GM) Place replaced the Coliseum for the NHL's Canucks in 1995, but the old building still has plenty of life in it. Some games of the 2006 World U20 (Junior) Championship were played at the Coliseum, and both figure skating and short-track speed-skating events were held there during the 2010 Olympic Winter Games. The arena is still used for the Vancouver Giants of the junior WHL.

GM Place was the new home for the Canucks starting in 1995, and it also was home for the short-lived Vancouver Grizzlies of the NBA (for six seasons). In the summer of 2010, the name of the arena was changed to Rogers Arena, although nothing else about the venue changed.

The building had a third name, albeit temporarily, during the Olympics, when it was called Canada Hockey Place (CHP) to avoid conflict of sponsorship with the International Olympic Committee.

Canada's Tessa Virtue and Scott Moir perform at the Pacific Coliseum during the 2010 Olympics.

HISTORY OF THE SWEATER

Although there have been many permutations and small changes to their logo and team sweater, the Canucks have used four principle designs since entering the NHL in 1970 (in all, there are thirteen different sweater designs in the team's NHL history).

The first was the classic stick inside a rink, designed by Joe Borovich, which lasted until 1978. The design originally included a large "V" on the sleeves, but this was removed after just one season.

In the summer of 1978, the Canucks introduced the large "V" design which included a yellow sweater and a black and red "V" logo for home games and a black sweater with a yellow and red "V" for road games. Designed by Beyl & Boyd of San Francisco, these were replaced in 1984.

The third design is often called the "skate logo" because it featured a stylized skate and the word "Canucks" underneath conveying motion. There were several variations to this design. As with the previous one, the home was primarily yellow and the road version black. In 1995, the home became white and the road was divided at a sharp angle into red on the upper half of the front and black on the lower half.

In 1997, the Canucks introduced what is their current logo featuring a killer whale breaking through the ice of a "C" (for Canucks). Various colours and interpretations have been employed, but this is the design that has endured the longest.

In 2008, the team also brought back the original, and much loved, stick-in-rink version as their vintage or third sweater.

Vancouver goalie Murray Wilson wearing the original togs.

Current forward Manny Malhotra wears the vintage version of the original.

Bill Derlago sports the "V"
sweater which lasted six years.

Igor Larionov wears
the "skate logo" which
succeeded the "V" edition.

Goalie Kevin Weekes wears the current
logo with killer whale emerging from
an icy "C".

Player	2010–11 Status
Andrew Alberts	Vancouver Canucks, NHL
Keith Ballard	Vancouver Canucks, NHL
Nolan Baumgartner	Manitoba Moose, AHL
Kevin Bieksa	Vancouver Canucks, NHL
Mario Bliznak	Manitoba Moose, AHL
Alexandre Bolduc	Manitoba/Vancouver
Alexandre Burrows	Vancouver Canucks, NHL
Guillaume Desbiens	Manitoba Moose, AHL
Alexander Edler	Vancouver Canucks, NHL
Christian Ehrhoff	Vancouver Canucks, NHL
Tanner Glass	Vancouver Canucks, NHL
Dan Hamhuis	Vancouver Canucks, NHL
Jannik Hansen	Vancouver Canucks, NHL
Darcy Hordichuk	traded to Florida, NHL
Ryan Kesler	Vancouver Canucks, NHL
Roberto Luongo	Vancouver Canucks, NHL
Manny Malhotra	Vancouver Canucks, NHL
Shane O'Brien	traded to Nashville, NHL
Victor Oreskovich	Manitoba/Vancouver
Joel Perrault	Manitoba/Vancouver
Travis Ramsey	Manitoba Moose, AHL
Mason Raymond	Vancouver Canucks, NHL
Aaron Rome	Vancouver Canucks, NHL
Marco Rosa	Manitoba Moose, AHL
Rick Rypien	Manitoba/Vancouver
Sami Salo	Vancouver Canucks, NHL
Mikael Samuelsson	Vancouver Canucks, NHL
Peter Schaefer	played for ERC Ingolstadt, DEL
Cory Schneider	Vancouver Canucks, NHL
Daniel Sedin	Vancouver Canucks, NHL
Henrik Sedin	Vancouver Canucks, NHL
David Shantz	played in ECHL
Sergei Shirokov	Manitoba Moose, AHL
Lee Sweatt	Manitoba Moose, AHL
Jeff Tambellini	Vancouver Canucks, NHL
Raffi Torres	Vancouver Canucks, NHL
Tyler Weiman	Manitoba Moose, AHL
Shawn Weller	Manitoba Moose, AHL
Sean Zimmerman	traded to Boston/ played in AHL

Daniel Sedin.

Like many a coach, Alain Vigneault started his life in hockey as a player, only to find he had limited skills compared to the wizards of the NHL. A rough and rugged defenceman, he played junior with Hull and Trois-Rivieres in the QMJHL and was drafted 161st overall by St. Louis in 1981. He played forty-two games for the Blues over the course of the next two years, but played mostly in the AHL until retiring just three years later.

Vigneault immediately became a scout for the Blues, serving in this capacity for two years before becoming head coach of the Trois-Rivieres team he played on just a few years earlier. He was only twenty-five years old at the time, and after one year he moved on to Hull. In his first year with the Olympiques, he took the team to the Memorial Cup and was named coach of the year in the QMJHL. He remained in junior hockey for the next four years. In 1992, he became an assistant coach for the Ottawa Senators, but in 1995 he returned to the QMJHL, this time with Beauport. In 1997, the Montreal Canadiens offered him the head coaching job.

Vigneault jumped at the chance, of course, but he lasted only three and a half years, going to the playoffs just once. He then returned to junior hockey, but in 2005 the Canucks offered him the head coaching job of their farm team in Manitoba. A year later, he was behind the bench for the Canucks, where he has been ever since.

Prior to the 2011 playoffs, the team had made the post-season three of four years with Vigneault, missing only in 2008. But the team had never made it past the second round and fans wondered if it would ever return to the Stanley Cup Final as it had in 1994 and 1982. Those questions have been laid to rest now, but Vigneault remains hungry for a Cup win that was so close and yet so far in 2011.

Atlantic Division

	GP	W	L	OT	GF	GA	Pts
Philadelphia	82	47	23	12	259	223	106
Pittsburgh	82	49	25	8	238	199	106
NY Rangers	82	44	33	5	233	198	93
New Jersey	82	38	39	5	174	209	81
NY Islanders	82	30	39	13	229	264	73

Northeast Division

	GP	W	L	OT	GF	GA	Pts
Boston	82	46	25	11	246	195	103
Montreal	82	44	30	8	216	209	96
Buffalo	82	43	29	10	245	229	96
Toronto	82	37	34	11	218	251	85
Ottawa	82	32	40	10	192	250	74

Southeast Division

	GP	W	L	OT	GF	GA	Pts
Washington	82	48	23	11	224	197	107
Tampa Bay	82	46	25	11	247	240	103
Carolina	82	40	31	11	236	239	91
Atlanta	82	34	36	12	223	269	80
Florida	82	30	40	12	195	229	72

Central Division

	GP	W	L	OT	GF	GA	Pts
Detroit	82	47	25	10	261	241	104
Nashville	82	44	27	11	219	194	99
Chicago	82	44	29	9	258	225	97
St. Louis	82	38	33	11	240	234	87
Columbus	82	34	35	13	215	258	81

Northwest Division

	GP	W	L	OT	GF	GA	Pts
Vancouver	82	54	19	9	262	185	117
Calgary	82	41	29	12	250	237	94
Minnesota	82	39	35	8	206	233	86
Colorado	82	30	44	8	227	288	68
Edmonton	82	25	45	12	193	269	62

Pacific Division

	GP	W	L	OT	GF	GA	Pts
San Jose	82	48	25	9	248	213	105
Anaheim	82	47	30	5	239	235	99
Phoenix	82	43	26	13	231	226	99
Los Angeles	82	46	30	6	219	198	98
Dallas	82	42	29	11	227	233	95

REGULAR SEASON RESULTS, 2010-11

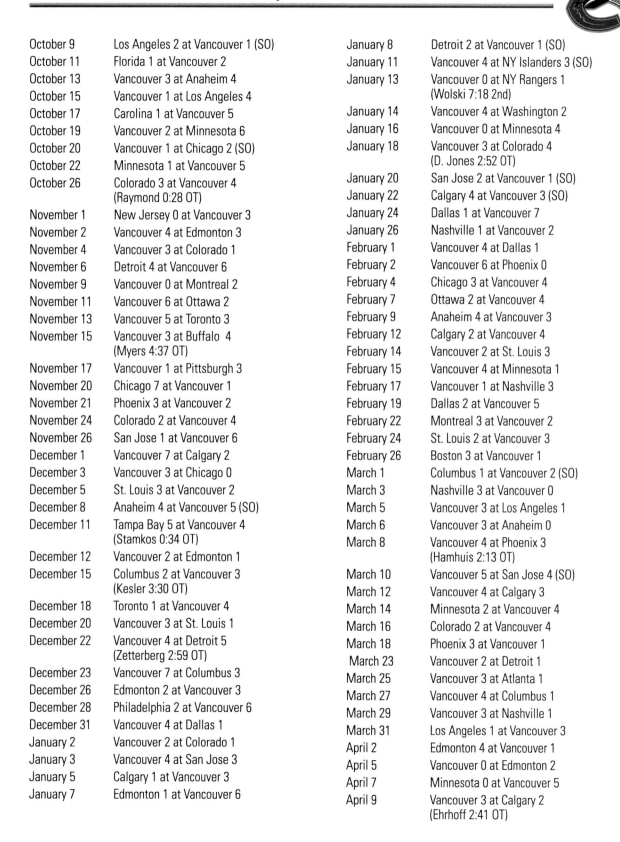

October 9	Los Angeles 2 at Vancouver 1 (SO)
October 11	Florida 1 at Vancouver 2
October 13	Vancouver 3 at Anaheim 4
October 15	Vancouver 1 at Los Angeles 4
October 17	Carolina 1 at Vancouver 5
October 19	Vancouver 2 at Minnesota 6
October 20	Vancouver 1 at Chicago 2 (SO)
October 22	Minnesota 1 at Vancouver 5
October 26	Colorado 3 at Vancouver 4 (Raymond 0:28 OT)
November 1	New Jersey 0 at Vancouver 3
November 2	Vancouver 4 at Edmonton 3
November 4	Vancouver 3 at Colorado 1
November 6	Detroit 4 at Vancouver 6
November 9	Vancouver 0 at Montreal 2
November 11	Vancouver 6 at Ottawa 2
November 13	Vancouver 5 at Toronto 3
November 15	Vancouver 3 at Buffalo 4 (Myers 4:37 OT)
November 17	Vancouver 1 at Pittsburgh 3
November 20	Chicago 7 at Vancouver 1
November 21	Phoenix 3 at Vancouver 2
November 24	Colorado 2 at Vancouver 4
November 26	San Jose 1 at Vancouver 6
December 1	Vancouver 7 at Calgary 2
December 3	Vancouver 3 at Chicago 0
December 5	St. Louis 3 at Vancouver 2
December 8	Anaheim 4 at Vancouver 5 (SO)
December 11	Tampa Bay 5 at Vancouver 4 (Stamkos 0:34 OT)
December 12	Vancouver 2 at Edmonton 1
December 15	Columbus 2 at Vancouver 3 (Kesler 3:30 OT)
December 18	Toronto 1 at Vancouver 4
December 20	Vancouver 3 at St. Louis 1
December 22	Vancouver 4 at Detroit 5 (Zetterberg 2:59 OT)
December 23	Vancouver 7 at Columbus 3
December 26	Edmonton 2 at Vancouver 3
December 28	Philadelphia 2 at Vancouver 6
December 31	Vancouver 4 at Dallas 1
January 2	Vancouver 2 at Colorado 1
January 3	Vancouver 4 at San Jose 3
January 5	Calgary 1 at Vancouver 3
January 7	Edmonton 1 at Vancouver 6
January 8	Detroit 2 at Vancouver 1 (SO)
January 11	Vancouver 4 at NY Islanders 3 (SO)
January 13	Vancouver 0 at NY Rangers 1 (Wolski 7:18 2nd)
January 14	Vancouver 4 at Washington 2
January 16	Vancouver 0 at Minnesota 4
January 18	Vancouver 3 at Colorado 4 (D. Jones 2:52 OT)
January 20	San Jose 2 at Vancouver 1 (SO)
January 22	Calgary 4 at Vancouver 3 (SO)
January 24	Dallas 1 at Vancouver 7
January 26	Nashville 1 at Vancouver 2
February 1	Vancouver 4 at Dallas 1
February 2	Vancouver 6 at Phoenix 0
February 4	Chicago 3 at Vancouver 4
February 7	Ottawa 2 at Vancouver 4
February 9	Anaheim 4 at Vancouver 3
February 12	Calgary 2 at Vancouver 4
February 14	Vancouver 2 at St. Louis 3
February 15	Vancouver 4 at Minnesota 1
February 17	Vancouver 1 at Nashville 3
February 19	Dallas 2 at Vancouver 5
February 22	Montreal 3 at Vancouver 2
February 24	St. Louis 2 at Vancouver 3
February 26	Boston 3 at Vancouver 1
March 1	Columbus 1 at Vancouver 2 (SO)
March 3	Nashville 3 at Vancouver 0
March 5	Vancouver 3 at Los Angeles 1
March 6	Vancouver 3 at Anaheim 0
March 8	Vancouver 4 at Phoenix 3 (Hamhuis 2:13 OT)
March 10	Vancouver 5 at San Jose 4 (SO)
March 12	Vancouver 4 at Calgary 3
March 14	Minnesota 2 at Vancouver 4
March 16	Colorado 2 at Vancouver 4
March 18	Phoenix 3 at Vancouver 1
March 23	Vancouver 2 at Detroit 1
March 25	Vancouver 3 at Atlanta 1
March 27	Vancouver 4 at Columbus 1
March 29	Vancouver 3 at Nashville 1
March 31	Los Angeles 1 at Vancouver 3
April 2	Edmonton 4 at Vancouver 1
April 5	Vancouver 0 at Edmonton 2
April 7	Minnesota 0 at Vancouver 5
April 9	Vancouver 3 at Calgary 2 (Ehrhoff 2:41 OT)

Eastern Conference Quarter-Final

(1) Washington vs. (8) NY Rangers

April 13   NY Rangers 1 at Washington 2
            (Semin 18:24 OT)
April 15   NY Rangers 0 at Washington 2 [Neuvirth]
April 17   Washington 2 at NY Rangers 3
April 20   Washington 4 at NY Rangers 3
            (Chimera 32:36 OT)
April 23   NY Rangers 1 at Washington 3

Washington wins best-of-seven 4-1

(2) Philadelphia vs. (7) Buffalo

April 14   Buffalo 1 at Philadelphia 0 [Miller]
April 16   Buffalo 4 at Philadelphia 5
April 18   Philadelphia 4 at Buffalo 2
April 20   Philadelphia 0 at Buffalo 1 [Miller]
April 22   Buffalo 4 at Philadelphia 3 (Ennis 5:31 OT)
April 24   Philadelphia 5 at Buffalo 4 (Leino 4:43 OT)
April 26   Buffalo 2 at Philadelphia 5

Philadelphia wins best-of-seven 4-3

(3) Boston vs. (6) Montreal

April 14   Montreal 2 at Boston 0 [Price]
April 16   Montreal 3 at Boston 1
April 18   Boston 4 at Montreal 2
April 21   Boston 5 at Montreal 4 (Ryder 1:59 OT)
April 23   Montreal 1 at Boston 2 (Horton 29:03 OT)
April 26   Boston 1 at Montreal 2
April 27   Montreal 3 at Boston 4 (Horton 5:43 OT)

Boston wins best-of-seven 4-3

(4) Pittsburgh vs. (5) Tampa Bay

April 13   Tampa Bay 0 at Pittsburgh 3 [Fleury]
April 15   Tampa Bay 5 at Pittsburgh 1
April 18   Pittsburgh 3 at Tampa Bay 2
April 20   Pittsburgh 3 at Tampa Bay 2 (Neal 23:38 OT)
April 23   Tampa Bay 8 at Pittsburgh 2
April 25   Pittsburgh 2 at Tampa Bay 4
April 27   Tampa Bay 1 at Pittsburgh 0 [Roloson]

Tampa Bay wins best-of-seven 4-3

Western Conference Quarter-Final

(1) Vancouver vs. (8) Chicago

April 13   Chicago 0 at Vancouver 2 [Luongo]
April 15   Chicago 3 at Vancouver 4
April 17   Vancouver 3 at Chicago 2
April 19   Vancouver 2 at Chicago 7
April 21   Chicago 5 at Vancouver 0 [Crawford]
April 24   Vancouver 3 at Chicago 4 (B. Smith 15:30 OT)
April 26   Chicago 1 at Vancouver 2 (Burrows 5:22 OT)

Vancouver wins best-of-seven 4-3

(2) San Jose vs. (7) Los Angeles

April 14   Los Angeles 2 at San Jose 3 (Pavelski 14:44 OT)
April 16   Los Angeles 4 at San Jose 0 [Quick]
April 17   San Jose 6 at Los Angeles 5
            (Setoguchi 3:09 OT)
April 21   San Jose 6 at Los Angeles 3
April 23   Los Angeles 3 at San Jose 1
April 25   San Jose 4 at Los Angeles 3
            (Thornton 2:22 OT)

San Jose wins best-of-seven 4-2

(3) Detroit vs. (6) Phoenix

April 13   Phoenix 2 at Detroit 4
April 16   Phoenix 3 at Detroit 4
April 18   Detroit 4 at Phoenix 2
April 20   Detroit 6 at Phoenix 3

Detroit wins best-of-seven 4-0

(4) Anaheim vs. (5) Nashville

April 13   Nashville 4 at Anaheim 1
April 15   Nashville 3 at Anaheim 5
April 17   Anaheim 3 at Nashville 4
April 20   Anaheim 6 at Nashville 3
April 22   Nashville 4 at Anaheim 3 (Smithson 1:57 OT)
April 24   Anaheim 2 at Nashville 4

Nashville wins best-of-seven 4-2

Eastern Conference Semi-Final
(1) Washington vs. (5) Tampa Bay

April 29	Tampa Bay 4 at Washington 2
May 1	Tampa Bay 3 at Washington 2 (Lecavalier 6:19 OT)
May 3	Washington 3 at Tampa Bay 4
May 4	Washington 3 at Tampa Bay 5

Tampa Bay wins best-of-seven 4-0

(2) Philadelphia vs. (3) Boston

April 30	Boston 7 at Philadelphia 3
May 2	Boston 3 at Philadelphia 2 (Krejci 14:00 OT)
May 4	Philadelphia 1 at Boston 5
May 6	Philadelphia 1 at Boston 5

Boston wins best-of-seven 4-0

Eastern Conference Final
(3) Boston vs. (5) Tampa Bay

May 14	Tampa Bay 5 at Boston 2
May 17	Tampa Bay 5 at Boston 6
May 19	Boston 2 at Tampa Bay 0 [Thomas]
May 21	Boston 3 at Tampa Bay 5
May 23	Tampa Bay 1 at Boston 3
May 25	Boston 4 at Tampa Bay 5
May 27	Tampa Bay 0 at Boston 1

Boston wins best-of-seven 4-3

Western Conference Semi-Final
(1) Vancouver vs. (5) Nashville

April 28	Nashville 0 at Vancouver 1 [Luongo]
April 30	Nashville 2 at Vancouver 1 (Halischuk 34:51 OT)
May 3	Vancouver 3 at Nashville 2 (Kesler 10:45 OT)
May 5	Vancouver 4 at Nashville 2
May 7	Nashville 4 at Vancouver 3
May 9	Vancouver 2 at Nashville 1

Vancouver wins best-of-seven 4-2

(2) San Jose vs. (3) Detroit

April 29	Detroit 1 at San Jose 2 (Ferriero 7:03 OT)
May 1	Detroit 1 at San Jose 2
May 4	San Jose 4 at Detroit 3 (Setoguchi 9:21 OT)
May 6	San Jose 3 at Detroit 4
May 8	Detroit 4 at San Jose 3
May 10	San Jose 1 at Detroit 3
May 12	Detroit 2 at San Jose 3

San Jose wins best-of-seven 4-3

Western Conference Final
(1) Vancouver vs. (2) San Jose

May 15	San Jose 2 at Vancouver 3
May 18	San Jose 3 at Vancouver 7
May 20	Vancouver 3 at San Jose 4
May 22	Vancouver 4 at San Jose 2
May 24	San Jose 2 at Vancouver 3 (Bieksa 30:18 OT)

Vancouver wins best-of-seven 4-1

Stanley Cup Final
(1) Vancouver vs. (3) Boston

June 1	Boston 0 at Vancouver 1 [Luongo]
June 4	Boston 2 at Vancouver 3 (Burrows 0:11 OT)
June 6	Vancouver 1 at Boston 8
June 8	Vancouver 0 at Boston 4 [Thomas]
June 10	Boston 0 at Vancouver 1 [Luongo]
June 13	Vancouver 2 at Boston 5
June 15	Boston 4 at Vancouver 0 [Thomas]

Boston wins best-of-seven 4-3

	GP	G	A	P	Pim
Daniel Sedin	82	41	63	104	32
Henrik Sedin	82	19	75	94	40
Ryan Kesler	82	41	32	73	66
Mikael Samuelsson	75	18	32	50	36
Christian Ehrhoff	79	14	36	50	52
Alexandre Burrows	72	26	22	48	77
Mason Raymond	70	15	24	39	10
Alexander Edler	51	8	25	33	24
Manny Malhotra	72	11	19	30	22
Raffi Torres	80	14	15	29	78
Jannik Hansen	82	9	20	29	32
Dan Hamhuis	64	6	17	23	34
Kevin Bieksa	66	6	16	22	73
Jeff Tambellini	62	9	8	17	18
Tanner Glass	73	3	7	10	72
Sami Salo	27	3	4	7	14
Keith Ballard	65	2	5	7	53
Andrew Alberts	42	1	6	7	41
Chris Higgins	14	2	3	5	6
Aaron Rome	56	1	4	5	53

	GP	G	A	P	Pim
Alexandre Bolduc	24	2	2	4	21
Victor Oreskovich	16	0	3	3	8
Roberto Luongo	60	0	3	3	2
Cory Schneider	25	0	3	3	0
Aaron Volpatti	15	1	1	2	16
Peter Schaefer	16	1	1	2	2
Lee Sweatt	3	1	1	2	2
Cody Hodgson	8	1	1	2	0
Maxim Lapierre	19	1	0	1	8
Mario Bliznak	4	1	0	1	0
Sergei Shirokov	2	1	0	1	0
Rick Rypien	9	0	1	1	31
Chris Tanev	29	0	1	1	0
Guillaume Desbiens	12	0	0	0	10
Joel Perrault	7	0	0	0	0
Jann Sauve	5	0	0	0	0
Jonas Andersson	4	0	0	0	0
Ryan Parent	4	0	0	0	0
Evan Oberg	2	0	0	0	0

In Goal

	GP	W-L-OT	Mins	GA	SO	GAA
Roberto Luongo	60	38-15-7	3,589:39	126	4	2.11
Cory Schneider	25	16-4-2	1,371:47	51	1	2.23

	GP	G	A	P	Pim
Henrik Sedin	25	3	19	22	16
Daniel Sedin	25	9	11	20	32
Ryan Kesler	25	7	12	19	47
Alexandre Burrows	25	9	8	17	34
Christian Ehrhoff	23	2	10	12	16
Alexander Edler	25	2	9	11	8
Kevin Bieksa	25	5	5	10	51
Jannik Hansen	25	3	6	9	18
Chris Higgins	25	4	4	8	2
Mason Raymond	24	2	6	8	6
Raffi Torres	23	3	4	7	28
Dan Hamhuis	19	1	5	6	6
Maxim Lapierre	25	3	2	5	56
Sami Salo	21	3	2	5	2

	GP	G	A	P	Pim
Mikael Samuelsson	11	1	2	3	8
Aaron Rome	14	1	0	1	37
Cody Hodgson	12	0	1	1	2
Tanner Glass	20	0	0	0	18
Victor Oreskovich	19	0	0	0	12
Keith Ballard	10	0	0	0	6
Andrew Alberts	9	0	0	0	6
Jeff Tambellini	6	0	0	0	2
Roberto Luongo	25	0	0	0	0
Manny Malhotra	6	0	0	0	0
Christopher Tanev	5	0	0	0	0
Cory Schneider	4	0	0	0	0
Alexandre Bolduc	3	0	0	0	0

In Goal

	GP	W-L-OT	Mins	GA	SO	GAA
Roberto Luongo	25	15-10	1,427:10	61	4	2.56
Cory Schneider	5	0-0	162:39	7	0	2.58

HOW THE TEAM WAS BUILT

By Draft

Kevin Bieksa
Selected 151st overall at 2001 Entry Draft

Mario Bliznak
Selected 205th overall at 2005 Entry Draft

Alexander Edler
Selected 91st overall at 2004 Entry Draft

Jannik Hansen
Selected 287th overall at 2004 Entry Draft

Cody Hodgson
Selected 10th overall at 2008 Entry Draft

Ryan Kesler
Selected 23rd overall at 2003 Entry Draft

Mason Raymond
Selected 51st overall at 2005 Entry Draft

Yann Sauve
Selected 41st overall at 2008 Entry Draft

Cory Schneider
Selected 26th overall at 2004 Entry Draft

Daniel Sedin
Selected 2nd overall at 1999 Entry Draft

Henrik Sedin
Selected 3rd overall at 1999 Entry Draft

Sergei Shirokov
Selected 163rd overall at 2006 Entry Draft

By Free Agent Signing

Alexandre Bolduc
Signed as a free agent on July 2, 2008

Alexandre Burrows
Signed as a free agent on November 8, 2005

Guillaume Desbiens
Signed as a free agent on July 22, 2009

Tanner Glass
Signed as a free agent on July 22, 2009

Dan Hamhuis
Signed as a free agent on July 1, 2010

Manny Malhotra
Signed as a free agent on July 1, 2010

Evan Oberg
Signed as a free agent on April 10, 2009

Joel Perrault
Signed as a free agent on July 1, 2010

Aaron Rome
Signed as a free agent on July 1, 2009

Rick Rypien
Signed as a free agent on November 9, 2005

Mikael Samuelsson
Signed as a free agent on July 3, 2009

Peter Schaefer
Signed as a free agent on October 7, 2010

Lee Sweatt
Signed as a free agent on May 31, 2010

Jeff Tambellini
Signed as a free agent on July 1, 2010

Chris Tanev
Signed as a free agent on May 31, 2010

Raffi Torres
Signed as a free agent on August 24, 2010

Aaron Volpatti
Signed as a free agent on March 22, 2010

By Trade

Andrew Alberts
Acquired from Carolina on March 3, 2010, for a 3rd-round draft choice in 2010

Jonas Andersson
Acquired from Nashville on October 5, 2010 with Ryan Parent for Shane O'Brien and Dan Gendur

Keith Ballard
Acquired from Florida on June 25, 2010, with Victor Oreskovich for Michael Grabner, Steve Bernier, and a 1st-round draft choice in 2010

Christian Ehrhoff
Acquired from San Jose on August 28, 2009 with Brad Lukowich for Patrick White and Daniel Rahimi

Chris Higgins
Acquired from Florida on February 28, 2011 for Evan Oberg and a 3rd-round draft choice in 2013

Maxim Lapierre
Acquired from Anaheim on February 28, 2011 with MacGregor Sharp for Joel Perrault and a 3rd-round draft choice in 2012

Roberto Luongo
Acquired from Florida on June 23, 2006, with Lukas Krajicek and a 6th-round draft choice for Bryan Allen, Alex Auld, and Todd Bertuzzi

Victor Oreskovich
Acquired from Florida on June 25, 2010, with Keith Ballard for Michael Grabner, Steve Bernier, and a 1st-round draft choice in 2010

Ryan Parent
Acquired from Nashville on October 5, 2010 with Jonas Andersson for Shane O'Brien and Dan Gendur

Sami Salo
Aquired from Ottawa on September 21, 2002 for Peter Schaefer

	GP	G	A	P	Pim		GP	G	A	P	Pim
Sergei Shirokov	76	22	36	58	51	Aaron Volpatti	53	2	9	11	74
Bill Sweatt	80	19	27	46	28	Chris Tanev	39	1	8	9	16
Mark Flood	63	11	29	40	29	Jeff Tambellini	7	5	2	7	0
Marco Rosa	51	13	21	34	20	Josh Aspenlind	22	0	5	5	26
Cody Hodgson	52	17	13	30	14	Tom Maxwell	39	4	0	4	60
Nolan Baumgartner	66	4	25	29	36	Ryan Cruthers	12	3	1	4	11
Jordan Schroeder	61	10	18	28	10	Stefan Schneider	47	2	2	4	9
Guillaume Desbiens	53	11	16	27	104	Keith Seabrook	15	1	2	3	8
Mario Bliznak	74	11	16	27	22	Sami Salo	3	2	0	2	2
Shawn Weller	67	12	11	23	50	Ryan Parent	39	1	1	2	56
Kevin Connauton	73	11	12	23	51	Ryan McGinnis	19	1	1	2	14
Joel Perrault	37	5	18	23	43	Jason Jaffray	6	1	1	2	2
Alexandre Bolduc	26	6	9	15	28	Rick Rypien	11	0	2	2	9
Kevin Clark	43	6	8	14	22	Eddie Lack	53	0	2	2	4
Lee Sweatt	41	5	9	14	18	Andy Brandt	5	0	2	2	0
Yann Sauve	39	3	11	14	24	Dusty Collins	3	1	0	1	12
Victor Oreskovich	40	4	8	12	38	Geoff Waugh	2	0	0	0	4
Travis Ramsey	57	0	12	12	63	Tyler Weiman	29	0	0	0	0
Garth Murray	55	6	5	11	90	Jason Pitton	1	0	0	0	2
Evan Oberg	38	6	5	11	28	Kyle Bushee	2	0	0	0	0
Jonas Andersson	20	5	6	11	16	Francis Lemieux	2	0	0	0	0

In Goal

	GP	W-L-OT	Mins	GA	SO	GAA
Eddie Lack	53	28-21-4	3,135	118	5	2.26
Tyler Weiman	29	15-10-2	1,717	75	1	2.62

GAME ONE — *April 13, 2011*

Chicago 0 at **Vancouver 2**

(Vancouver leads series 1-0)

Playing Chicago to start the playoffs was double whammy for the Canucks. Chicago had eliminated Vancouver in each if the previous two playoffs, both times in six games, and the Hawks were reigning Stanley Cup champions. On the flip side, the Canucks had home-ice advantage and the Hawks had changed more than half their roster the previous summer, so it wasn't quite the same team.

Either way, this game was decided by timely scoring in the first period for Vancouver and timely goaltending from Roberto Luongo in the final forty minutes. The goalie recorded his second career playoff shutout. The Canucks got on the board just seven minutes into the game when Kevin Bieksa's point shot was deflected in front by Chris Higgins and over the glove of goalie Corey Crawford.

Less than three-and-a-half minutes later, the Canucks got what little cushion they would need. The play started in the Vancouver end when Ryan Kesler blocked a shot and Mikael Samuelsson fed Jannik Hansen a breakaway pass. There was a broken stick lying in the slot directly in front of Crawford, but Hansen fired a great shot just before he reached the discarded twig, fooling the goalie and making it a 2–0 game for the home side.

"He made a quick move and I thought I might have had my glove close to him enough, but he got it up pretty quick," Crawford said of the shot.

As big as the two goals were, the up-tempo first period also featured several big hits, the Canucks establishing a physical game that Chicago couldn't match. Late in the first period veteran blue-liner Sami Salo caught Tomas Kopecky with his head down, nailing him with a clean check and forcing the Hawks forward to the dressing room for the rest of the night.

"It was fantastic," Luongo said of the team's great start. "Not only the fact that we scored, but our physical presence on the forecheck was huge. Guys had some big hits. That really set a good pace and tempo for our team."

Roberto Luongo stopped this and every other shot that came his way in a game one, 2-0 win over Chicago.

22

Conference Quarter-Final — Vancouver Canucks vs. Chicago Blackhawks

Vancouver's Alexandre Burrows (right) fights for position against Chicago's Nick Leddy.

The Hawks had three power-play chances over the final two periods but they couldn't beat Luongo, and the defence showed a commitment to getting in the way of as many shots as possible. But as Luongo said after, "It doesn't really mean anything at the end of the day if we don't win the series. That's what it is all about. We won game one, which is nice, but we still have a lot of work to do and we're not going to get ahead of ourselves here."

This tempered enthusiasm was the result of experience, the Canucks having won the first game in both previous years against the Hawks, only to lose both series. This year seemed different, though. The Canucks looked to be the hungrier and more determined team. If they kept up this pace, the outcome was in their hands.

Conference Quarter-Final — Vancouver Canucks vs. Chicago Blackhawks

23

GAME TWO — *April 15, 2011*

Chicago 3 at **Vancouver 4**

(Vancouver leads series 2–0)

The Canucks accomplished tonight what they hadn't the two previous series against Chicago—jump to a 2–0 series lead. They did so through grit and determination, with their star players outperforming the Hawks' star players. In the end, Daniel Sedin led the way with two goals and an assist while Chicago captain Jonathan Toews was held off the scoresheet again.

Jannik Hansen got the only goal of the first, going from goat to hero in the blink of an eye. He took the game's first penalty to put his team in a hole, but the penalty killers did a terrific job of keeping the puck to the outside on the Chicago power play. Hansen stepped out of the box and into the rush, and Daniel Sedin fed him a great pass from behind the Hawks' net as Hansen reached the top of the faceoff circle. He blew a shot past Crawford, and the Canucks went to the dressing room with a 1–0 lead.

Daniel made it a 2–0 game early in the second period, and although there was still plenty of time left on the clock, psychologically it was a significant inspiration to the team. It came on a power play after a Patrick Sharp penalty late in the second period carried over, and playing on fresh ice the Canucks were able to move the puck around crisply before Daniel's shot beat Corey Crawford just thirty seconds into the middle period.

The Hawks, however, continued to press and made it a 2–1 game midway through the period thanks to Ben Smith. But the Hawks did something uncharacteristic and let up as the period drew to a close. Alexander Edler let go a point shot that Smith tipped in front of his own goalie and, with less than four seconds left on the clock, the Canucks restored their two-goal lead.

A downcast group of Hawks took the ice to start the third period, still trailing after forty minutes of

Last year's Conn Smythe Trophy winner Jonathan Toews of Chicago takes a faceoff against current Art Ross Trophy winner Henrik Sedin.

Vancouver's Ryan Kesler makes life difficult for Chicago goalie Corey Crawford.

Conference Quarter-Final — Vancouver Canucks vs. Chicago Blackhawks

25

Roberto Luongo flashes the glove while Brent Seabrook looks for a rebound that doesn't come.

play. But Viktor Stalberg's shot early in the third beat Luongo, again cutting the Vancouver lead to one and swinging the momentum back to the Hawks.

Just past the midway mark of the period, though, the see-saw battle saw Daniel get his second goal of the night on a nice wrist shot from the left faceoff circle, restoring for a third time the team's two-goal lead.

"They're not the Stanley Cup champions for nothing," Luongo said. "We didn't expect them to keel over or roll over there. They were coming strong and obviously Danny scored a huge goal for us."

Smith made it 4–3 at 12:50, and the end of the game was peculiar in that the final six minutes were played without a whistle. Chicago was unable to slow the game down or set plays, call a timeout or regroup. Vancouver played flawless defence, and the referees helped out by calling not a single penalty in the final period. In fact, in the whole game both teams had only two minors as the officials let the teams decide the game through good, old-fashioned five-on-five hockey.

"Sometimes it's not always about playing with the lead," said Chicago's captain Jonathan Toews. "It's not going to be a perfect game, especially on the road. We just kept giving them consistent scoring chances and let them run away with the game. Every time you get a goal and try to come back, you pull within one, you get momentum and we just found ways to give it back to them."

GAME THREE — *April 17, 2011*
Vancouver 3 at Chicago 2
(Vancouver leads series 3–0)

One of the reasons Vancouver signed Mikael Samuelsson in the summer of 2009 was that general manager Mike Gillis knew Samuelsson was a winner, well trained in playoff hockey by the Detroit Red Wings. Well, it was a Samuelsson goal early in the third period that broke a 2–2 tie and gave the Canucks a huge 3–0 series lead, a lead almost too good to be true. It wasn't vintage, pretty hockey, but it got the job done, and the scoreboard allows no marks for aesthetics.

The game started out favourably for the home side as the Hawks got the only goal of the first period and dominated the play. The only reason they were leading by only a single goal after twenty minutes was either a lack of scoring touch or great goaltending from Roberto Luongo, depending on one's perspective.

Duncan Keith opened the scoring at 6:54 on the power play, and soon after the Hawks had a two-man advantage for 1:17. That's when Luongo stepped up and made great saves on captain Jonathan Toews, linemate Patrick Kane, and lastly Patrick Sharp to frustrate the home side and give the visitors a huge morale boost heading to the dressing room.

"The game could have been over there early on," said captain Henrik Sedin of the Canucks. "If they score there, their big guns get confidence and that's a tough battle for us. But, he made some huge saves for us and that's a boost for the bench."

Roberto Luongo catches a fluttering puck that almost hits teammate Maxim Lapierre.

Defenceman Alexander Edler tries to clear Jonathan Toews from the front of the Vancouver goal.

Vancouver struck for two goals just fifty-four seconds apart midway through the second period. Christian Ehrhoff tied the score with a shot from the point on the power play that evaded a clump of bodies in front and went past a helpless Corey Crawford, and then Daniel Sedin wired a pass from Alexander Edler to make it 2–1.

Controversy erupted less than two minutes later. Vancouver's Raffi Torres, playing for the first time since serving a four-game suspension for an elbow to the head of Edmonton's Jordan Eberle, crushed Brent Seabrook behind the Chicago goal and received a minor penalty. Chicago coach Joel Quenneville saw the hit as dirty and wanted a harsher punishment, but Alain Vigneault thought it a hard, but clean, "hockey hit," as they say.

The Hawks tied the game on the ensuing power play, Sharp converting a nice pass from Toews, leaving the third period to decide matters. The Hawks should have been the more desperate team. After all, the prospects for a series win after falling behind 3–0 were slim to none, yet the Canucks got the only goal of the period.

Samuelsson's goal came off a scramble. Christian Ehrhoff and Henrik Sedin both had shots that were stopped in front, but the loose puck fell right to Samuelsson who had an empty net to work with. "He was out of position," Samuelsson said of goalie Crawford. "I'll take it any day."

"We battled," said Vancouver's Kevin Bieksa. "It wasn't a perfect game. It wasn't pretty, but sometimes on the road in the playoffs you need a couple of ugly ones. The main thing is we were resilient. We were down, we were up, they tied it, there was a lot of momentum shifts and we stuck with it."

Daniel Sedin celebrates his second-period goal that gave the Canucks a 2-1 lead.

GAME FOUR — *April 19, 2011*

Vancouver 2 at **Chicago 7**

(Vancouver leads series 3–1)

The game was tied 1–1 before it was even five minutes old, but Chicago scored six consecutive goals to coast to a 7–2 win, with a late Canucks goal making the score marginally closer. It was a blowout because Vancouver took its foot off its collective pedal, and it proved to be a costly lapse.

"It's not very often this year after a game that I've said that we got outworked by the opposition, but we got outworked tonight," offered Vancouver coach Alain Vigneault. "We're going to park this one, turn the page on it, and get ready for the next one. We know the adjustments we need to make are real simple."

The game got out of hand in the third period. First, Patrick Sharp scored early to make it a 6–1 game, and then the teams got nasty, as often happens when a game is over and done with on the scoreboard. The

Canucks took four ten-minute misconducts in the third and Chicago two, and late in the game Kevin Bieksa fought Viktor Stalberg. In all, referees handed out eighty-eight penalty minutes in the final period.

Front and centre this evening, though, was Chicago's Dave Bolland. He had missed the previous six weeks with a concussion, failed his baseline test a week previous, but was cleared by doctors to play on the morning of the game. Yet he led the attack with a goal and three assists and was a plus-4. On the other side of the puck, the Sedins were held off the scoresheet.

"I knew I was ready," said a joyous Bolland, both for the win and his own health and performance. "I knew once I did the test and the doctor said I was okay I was ready to go. You don't want to get in too quick with these things because you never know what is going to happen, but I knew my head was 100 per cent and tonight was my night to come back."

Bryan Bickell scored 1:43 into the game to get the

Henrik Sedin (left) and Duncan Keith battle along the boards deep in the Chicago end.

Goalie Roberto Luongo clears the puck just as Jonathan Toews tries to beat him to it.

Chicago crowd into the game, but Sami Salo scored on a power play just three minutes later to tie the game. The rest of the period was evenly played, but Chicago came out the more desperate team in the second and was rewarded, scoring the only four goals of the period.

After Chicago made it 6–1 early in the third, Vigneault gave Roberto Luongo the rest of the night off and inserted backup Cory Schneider. "I don't think you can say it was Luongo's struggles—I think you can say it was Canucks' struggles," said Kevin Bieksa.

"I don't think you can pin tonight's loss on one guy. I don't think anyone is happy with their performance, so we shoulder that as a team."

The Canucks weren't panicking, though, because they were going home for game five, ahead 3–1 in the series. But as coach Joel Quenneville of the Hawks noted with prescient care: "I know there is a tougher challenge going forward in Vancouver, but we're just happy to have the momentum. We felt there was no pressure on us going into today's game and that's not going to change."

GAME FIVE —*April 21, 2011*

Chicago 5 at Vancouver 0
(Vancouver leads series 3–2)

Momentum is such a finicky bedfellow. One day, one minute, it's with you; the next minute, it isn't. Vancouver was in control of the series to such an extent that domination is the only appropriate epithet. Two games later, the best epithet was desperate.

All the elements that had contributed to the Canucks winning the first three games of the series had gone into reverse. Goalie Roberto Luongo was struggling to see the puck; the Sedins were more or less invisible; the team play was all but gone. And confidence? None left.

Chicago scored two goals early and added a third later in the first period, and that was pretty much the game right there. When Vancouver coach Alain Vigneault gave Luongo the hook for the second straight game after the Hawks made it 4–0 early in the second, the crowd cheered mockingly and the goalie's imperviousness was now seriously doubted by the confident Blackhawks.

Corey Crawford of the Hawks also played well when he had to, blocking all thirty-six shots he faced to earn his first career playoff shutout.

It didn't have to be like this. Chicago's Brian Campbell took a penalty only sixteen seconds after the opening faceoff, but the Canucks couldn't score and three minutes later, Tanner Glass reciprocated

The Hawks dominated game five to such an extent that Vancouver coach Alain Vigneault replaced number-one goalie Roberto Luongo with backup Cory Schneider early in the second period.

32

Conference Quarter-Final — Vancouver Canucks vs. Chicago Blackhawks

Mason Raymond does a superb job of screening Chicago goalie Corey Crawford.

when he took an interference penalty for Vancouver. Marian Hossa connected to give the visitors a 1–0 lead, and while Canucks fans squirmed uneasily, Duncan Keith made it 2–0 just twenty-four seconds later on a slapshot Luongo would have liked a second chance on. All the goals, though, had one thing in common—bodies in front of Luongo to make it hard for him to see the puck or make a clean save.

Patrick Kane extricated himself from a series-long scoring slump by tipping in a Sharp point shot at 12:17 to score his first goal of the post-season, and the Canucks, with plenty of time still left, seemed down and out already. They had no response for Chicago's new-found zip.

"Everybody can do more," coach Vigneault acknowledged. "I can do better and each and every one of our players can do better. That's what we're going to work on."

Perhaps the most impressive member of the Canucks was goalie Luongo. Despite being shelled the last two games, he still carried himself with a veteran's confidence after the game. "I've been at the top of my game for the last five months," he boasted. "I feel good in what I've been doing. You don't lose something like that in a game or two. To me, nothing changes. I'm going to be focused."

More worrisome, though, was Chicago's spirit of hope, made all the richer by last year's Philadelphia comeback against Boston. The Flyers were only the third team ever to complete a 3–0 comeback, eliminating Boston in game seven and eventually moving on to the Stanley Cup Final.

"We put ourselves in such a hole, but we'll take what Philly did last year and we'll give it a shot, see where it takes us," said Chicago blue-liner Brian Campbell.

The calm Daniel Sedin can't believe what he's seeing as his Canucks go down to a one-sided, 5-0, loss.

34

Conference Quarter-Final — Vancouver Canucks vs. Chicago Blackhawks

GAME SIX —*April 24, 2011*

Vancouver 3 at **Chicago** 4
(series tied 3–3)

The storylines were starting to pile up and the tension was getting thick. A once piece-of-cake series now had a tight noose around the collective necks of the Vancouver Canucks, who lost for the third straight game. Chicago, once down and out, was now part of history, having rallied to tie the series 3–3. The teams headed to Vancouver for a winner-take-all game thanks to the heroics of Ben Smith. He had scored twice in game two and tonight scored the overtime winner despite playing all but six games of the regular season with the Hawks' farm team in Rockford.

But the greatest surprise in the game was that coach Alain Vigneault of Vancouver decided to start backup goalie Cory Schneider and leave Roberto Luongo on the bench. The move backfired in two ways. First, Schneider injured himself and had to be replaced in the third period by Luongo. And second, because the team still lost.

"Sometimes you've just got to go with your gut," Vigneault said. "Sometimes the book is over rated. My gut told me it was the right thing to do."

Playing before a raucous crowd in Chicago, the Canucks started off strongly, scoring just 2:06 into the game when Daniel Sedin, invisible in the previous two games, scored on a wraparound that fooled goalie Corey Crawford.

Michael Frolik beats Cory Schneider on a penalty shot, and Schneider, injured on the play, is forced to leave the game.

Conference Quarter-Final — Vancouver Canucks vs. Chicago Blackhawks

35

A big-time collision along the boards sees Vancouver's Jannik Hansen collide with Niklas Hjalmarsson.

36

Conference Quarter-Final — Vancouver Canucks vs. Chicago Blackhawks

A scrum of seven players in front of the Vancouver goal battle rugby-style for position.

It wasn't until 14:57 that Bryan Bickell tied the game for Chicago, beating Schneider with a quick shot, but Alexandre Burrows put Vancouver up again, 2–1, at 18:48. The Canucks headed to the dressing room with a road lead after twenty minutes, playing their best hockey in a week.

The Hawks scored the only goal of the second, but it could have been worse for Vancouver. The team was down two men for 1:43 in the middle part of the period but killed off the disadvantage. It wasn't until 15:08 that Dave Bolland tied the game and sent the teams to their respective dressing rooms in a 2–2 game.

Again, though, Vancouver took the lead, their third of the game, thanks to a Kevin Bieksa goal just fifty-eight seconds into the third period. But Michael Frolik tied it for a third time at 2:31 on a penalty shot. Frolik scored with a great deke and high shot over the sprawling Schneider. The goalie fell awkwardly on the play and hurt his groin, and that was when Luongo was forced into action. The tense third period saw him face only two shots, but he was tested more often in the overtime that followed.

The winner came on a Luongo weakness, a rebound.

When he is on his game, the big goalie gobbles up every puck in his crease, but when he isn't, he is often weak with the loose pucks. Late in the first overtime period, Niklas Hjalmarsson's routine point shot wasn't handled cleanly by Luongo, and Smith, falling to the ice, managed to scoop it over a sprawled goalie to give Chicago the win and force a seventh game.

"I really just wanted to get to the front of the net," a jubilant Smith said of the winning play. "That's what I try and do. That's my game, to be a body in front of the net and whack at rebounds. Nik Hjalmarsson made a great, hard shot and the rebound bounced right there for me."

"Maybe that was a good thing," Frolik said of Vancouver's forced goalie change. "We got some good shots on Luongo after that, and he gave us a rebound."

Again, it was Luongo who wasn't panicking, only trying to keep a level head. "The same way Chicago did," he said when asked about how the team would handle game seven. "They were down 3–0 and came back and played a hell of a game and beat us 7–2, so they found a way. Now it's our turn to respond."

GAME SEVEN — *April 26, 2011*

Chicago 1 at **Vancouver 2**
*(**Vancouver** wins series 4–3)*

In one of the most dramatic finishes you'll ever see in a playoff game, the Vancouver Canucks did two things in one on this night. They eliminated Chicago and moved on to the Conference Semi-final—and they didn't blow a 3–0 series lead. But they did blow a lead late in the game before winning in overtime.

"This is what legends are made of," said a jubilant Vancouver goalie Roberto Luongo. "Game seven, OT. It doesn't get any better than that. Somebody is going to become a hero."

He would know. Only a year and a half ago he was in goal for the most important overtime in Canadian

hockey history, the gold-medal game of the 2010 Olympics. And like that night, when Sidney Crosby was the hero, Luongo watched as Alexandre Burrows made himself the hero, scoring both Canucks' goals, one early and that OT gem.

Vancouver entered the game with home-ice advantage, but given the pressure of not wanting to blow a 3–0 series lead, it might have felt like home-ice disadvantage. But Burrows contributed to a great Vancouver start by scoring the opening goal just 2:43 into the game, his hard one-timer from a perfect feed from Ryan Kesler beating Corey Crawford in the Chicago goal.

What seemed like a big early goal started to look more and more like the game winner as the night proceeded. Both goalies had their best games of

Roberto Luongo covers the low part of the net while teammate Christian Ehrhoff watches Dave Bolland in behind.

Henrik Sedin tries to beat Corey Crawford from a bad angle.

the series, and neither side could score. The referees called only three minors all game, and it seemed the game might well end 1–0.

Vancouver had a sensational chance to make it 2–0 early in the third period, though. Burrows was tripped on a breakaway and awarded a penalty shot just twenty-one seconds into the final period, but Crawford snapped his blocker in the way of the shot and the game stayed 1–0.

The Hawks seemed to run out of chances at 16:43 of the period when Duncan Keith took a hooking penalty. If the Canucks could kill off this power play, they'd be a little over one minute away from victory.

But the incredible happened. Jonathan Toews got his first goal of the series, short-handed no less, poking the puck home while on his knees and just 1:56 left in the game.

"The play he made on the tying goal, not a lot of guys in the League can do that," Luongo said. "That's why he won the Conn Smythe, was the MVP in the Olympics. It's a massive play by him and that's why he's the leader of the team."

That sent the game into a fourth period, and Burrows again figured prominently—twice. First, he took a holding penalty twenty-four seconds into the extra period, giving the Hawks a tremendous opportunity to win. The Canucks rallied around their net, though, allowed only one shot, and got back to even strength. Just three minutes later, Burrows caught Chris Campoli's clearing pass, controlled the puck, and went in on goal, beating Crawford to the stick side and sending the Canucks to the next round.

"I just dropped it and I knew the puck was rolling, so I wanted just to make sure it was going on net," Burrows described. "Those are tough shots to stop for goalies. It knuckled right through his blocker and went in."

A disconsolate Crawford, one of the stars of the night, took little solace in his great performance. "I was just trying to keep us in [the game]," he said. "I felt we would get our chance and eventually bury one. We did and had a lot of momentum heading into overtime. We had some chances in overtime and [Luongo] made some big stops. They got a lucky bounce, came streaking into the slot…it's tough to lose."

And so the Canucks slayed the demons by eliminating a team that had done the same to them the last two years. They had beaten a team that had made an historic rally, but that was a small victory in the big picture.

Said Luongo: "It's only the first round, and that's the crazy thing. We'll take this one tonight, enjoy it, but we know we've got another huge series coming up here."

Players mob Alexandre Burrows after his overtime goal gives Vancouver the series win.

40

Conference Quarter-Final — Vancouver Canucks vs. Chicago Blackhawks

GAME ONE — *April 28, 2011*

Nashville 0 at **Vancouver 1**

(Vancouver leads series 1–0)

Although this was game one of a new series, it was like game eight of the previous series in terms of the Vancouver Canucks' emotions. Having dispatched the Blackhawks only two nights previous in overtime, they were running on adrenaline this night. And, like the Chicago series, the team started with a shutout from Roberto Luongo and a game-winning goal from Chris Higgins. The 1–0 win, though, was flattering to the Predators, whom both coaches admitted were outplayed by a wide margin this night.

"I thought we'd be ready. I thought we had a pretty good idea of what was going to come at us, but we need everybody," Nashville coach Barry Trotz said in

a controlled tone later. "We win and lose as a group of twenty every night, and we had way too many passengers. Especially at this high level of competition in the second round, you can't play the way we did. We had a couple of games in the playoffs where we were on the other side and won all the fifty-fifty pucks. Tonight we didn't win any of those, especially up front. Let's be honest—we didn't deserve to win this hockey game."

Just as in the final game of the Chicago–Vancouver series, the two best players on the ice were the goalies, although Pekka Rinne was by far the busier of the two, stopping 29 of 30 shots. Luongo had to stop only 20, mostly harmless, and most in the third period when the Predators mounted their only serious offense.

Higgins scored at 12:14 of the second period, taking a pass from Maxim Lapierre after Lapierre had forced

Ryan Kesler looks for a pass in front of Nashville goalie Pekka Rinne.

Conference Semi-Final — Vancouver Canucks vs. Nashville Predators

41

Rinne to commit to him. Higgins had only to get the puck high into the open net with the goalie down and out, and he did. Shots at the time favoured Vancouver, 24–8, a clear indicator of how much the better team they were this night.

The Predators had two great chances to tie the game in the third. About five minutes in, Mike Fisher had a breakaway, but Luongo came out to challenge the shooter and Fisher drilled it in Luongo's logo.

"He was coming down, but two guys were on his back," Luongo said. "I kind of had a feeling he was going to shoot, so I just stepped up on him at the last second and pushed out toward his stick, tried to take away as much net as possible."

Then, late in the third, defenceman Shea Weber had an open net but fired one of his trademark bullet shots over top of the net.

Said Luongo: "Obviously game seven is not the same as a game one, but it's still the playoffs and you want to win the first one and set a good tempo for the rest of the series. No doubt the pressure level is not the same—but at the same time, every game is so important, as we discussed prior to the series."

Neither team scored on five power-play chances, but the Canucks controlled the puck impressively with the extra man while Nashville generated few shots when even one decent chance might have made a difference in the game.

Daniel Sedin tries to control the puck while Pekka Rinne slides across and blocks that side of the net.

Mason Raymond skates into the Nashville end trying to beat defenceman Shea Weber one-on-one.

Conference Semi-Final — Vancouver Canucks vs. Nashville Predators

43

GAME TWO — *April 30, 2011*
Nashville 2 at Vancouver 1
(Series tied 1–1)

For the second time in three games, the Canucks couldn't hold a lead late in the game, but while they rallied to win game seven against Chicago in overtime, they weren't so fortunate tonight. The result was that a 1–0 game turned into a 2–1 loss, and a 2–0 series lead turned into a 1–1 series tie with Nashville earning home-ice advantage.

The result could be expected in some ways because the Canucks had played so much high-intensity, pressure hockey in the last ten days, something was going to have to give. And truth be told, it was a little harder for them to get motivated against the Predators than for the Blackhawks, a team with a much richer league history and much more volatile history against the Canucks in recent years. But now the Canucks knew they had a series on their hands and this team from Tennessee wanted to eliminate them from the playoffs.

Pekka Rinne was better than Roberto Luongo, and the Predators capitalized on their chances while the Canucks mounted little offense and couldn't get the job done. Ryan Suter scored the tying goal with only sixty-seven seconds left in regulation and Rinne on the bench for an extra attacker. It came on a smart but fluky play, and one that has historically caused problems for Luongo.

Henrik Sedin comes out front from behind the Nashville goal, setting off a chain of events which creates havoc in the crease area.

Henrik Sedin gives David Legwand a facewash as the Nashville forward goes to the net with the puck.

A memorable collision from the 2011 playoffs sees Vancouver's Aaron Rome go down and Nashville's Jerred Smithson go up.

Suter was behind the Vancouver goal when he flipped the puck in front. It bounced off the goalie and in, a harmless-looking play, to be sure, but Luongo is known for having a tough time finding the puck from behind his own red line. The goal was the first for the Predators in the series after going nearly 119 minutes without one.

"I was just trying to get a whistle," Suter explained. "I knew there wasn't much time left. I just wanted to get it on him and hopefully he would've covered it. Then we could've drawn up a face-off play or something. I got a fortunate bounce there and it went in."

Up until that goal, the Canucks were riding a short-handed goal from Alexandre Burrows to the victory circle. That goal came two minutes into the second period. He skated into the Nashville end on a one-on-one situation, Shea Weber dealing with him. Burrows took a shot that went off Weber's skate, and he snapped a quick second shot before the defenceman could find the puck. It surprised Rinne as well.

It was a fortuitous lead, to say the least. Nashville had the better of play for most of the sixty minutes and outshot Vancouver 36–15 in regulation time. The overtime was just the opposite as Vancouver had the better chances but Nashville got the only goal.

Late in the first period Rinne had his best moment. Daniel Sedin was to his left and made a great cross-ice pass to Kevin Bieksa. His one-timer was headed in when Rinne leapt from side to side to make the best save of the playoffs and keep the score tied.

"Obviously, I was a little bit fortunate," Rinne said, downplaying his contributions to the win. "Sedin made a nice pass to Bieksa and I was able to get my blocker and my stick over there."

Matt Halischuk got the winner at 14:51 of the second overtime on a perfectly executed three-on-two off the rush. Nick Spaling set him up with a pass, and from the high slot Halischuk ripped a shot over Luongo's glove. "I kind of picked my spot," Spaling said. "Luckily it went in."

GAME THREE — *May 3, 2011*

Vancouver 3 at Nashville 2

(Vancouver leads series 2–1)

For the third time in four games, the Canucks allowed a late goal in the third period to rob the team of a win in regulation, but for the second of those three games they rallied to win in overtime. Tonight Ryan Kesler was the hero, scoring at 10:45 of the fourth period on the power play and spoiling another sensational game by Predators' goalie Pekka Rinne. Indeed, Kesler was the dominant player all night long, having a hand in all Vancouver goals. More important, the road win restored Vancouver's home-ice advantage, now leading 2–1 in the series with two home games remaining, if necessary.

The low-scoring series had a total of just nine goals so far in three games and twelve periods of hockey, the Canucks scoring five. In the first period, they were unlucky to be trailing 1–0 after a tenacious and impressive start in Nashville's building, coming out with a determination that caught the home Predators off-guard. But the only score of the period came from David Legwand on a short-handed goal.

Defenceman Alexander Edler was behind his own goal when Legwand stripped him of the puck. Edler hooked him trying to get it back, and a delayed penalty was in effect when Legwand passed to Nick Spaling in the corner. Spaling hit a charging Ryan Suter who spotted Legwand open in front, and he had an open net to make it 1–0 despite his team being outshot 10–2 at this point.

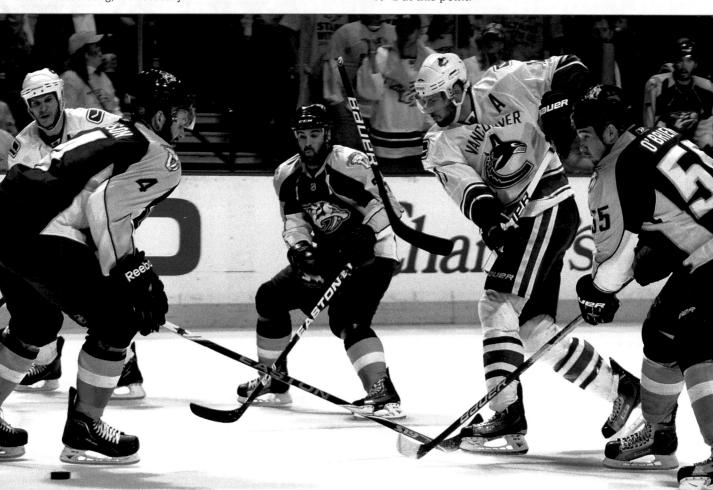

Ryan Kesler lets go a shot only to have his stick snap in half.

Traffic in front of goalie Pekka Rinne is heavy and physical as the goalie reaches around for the puck.

Conference Semi-Final — Vancouver Canucks vs. Nashville Predators

Henrik Sedin (left) and Ryan Kesler celebrate a Vancouver goal.

Edler didn't see any more power-play time, but that turned out to be a blessing in disguise on Kesler's winner.

Kesler got his first goal of the game and series at 1:00 of the second period, also on the power play from a late penalty in the first period by Jerred Smithson. The play started with Christian Ehrhoff carrying the puck into the Nashville end. Instead of curling and stopping at the blue-line to set up the man advantage, he continued down the wing, outwaited Rinne, and fired a pass to the back side where Kesler was standing, unattended. He had no problem converting the excellent pass.

The Canucks then took their first lead of the game early in the final period, and again Kesler was involved. The puck carrier, Chris Higgins, was knocked into Rinne by one of Nashville's defencemen, Shane

O'Brien. Kesler got to the loose puck, fired a pass back to Higgins who rifled a shot in.

Joel Ward tied the game at 13:18 when his pass in front hit a skate and went under Luongo's pad. In the overtime, Kesler first drew the penalty to Shea Weber for hooking and then, forty seconds later, he tipped a point shot from Mikael Samuelsson past Rinne. Normally Edler would have been at that point, but not after his first-period gaffe.

Explained coach Alain Vigneault in two easy sentences: "Eddie [Edler] lost the puck and it ended up in the back of our net. Easy call."

The hooking call, meanwhile, caused some discussion after the game. Nashville suggested it was a marginal call for an overtime situation, while Vancouver agreed with it. Said Kesler, simply: "He was hooking me. I thought it was a good call."

Conference Semi-Final — Vancouver Canucks vs. Nashville Predators

49

GAME FOUR — *May 5, 2011*
Vancouver 4 at **Nashville 2**
(Vancouver leads series 3–1)

Finally, the Vancouver Canucks ended a game in regulation with a strong final half of the third period, breaking a 2–2 tie by scoring the last two goals of the game and winning 4–2. The victory gave them a 3–1 series lead and a chance to eliminate the Predators two nights later, at home. And, for the second straight game, the dominant player was Ryan Kesler who had a goal and two assists and made several other important plays in his own end.

"He's getting some room," Predators coach Barry Trotz admitted of Kesler. "He's winning more battles and he's finding the net for them. I think in the first series he didn't have anything going for him. Right now, he's their best player, bar none."

The best news for the Canucks was that they were finally scoring some goals and finding ways to beat goalie Pekka Rinne, who had allowed only five goals through the first three games against the highest-scoring team in the league during the regular season. On the troubling side, Vancouver let slip two leads before rallying for the win, but that's as much a credit to the perseverance of the pesky Predators as to any weakness at the Canucks end of the ice.

Christian Ehrhoff scored the game's first goal late in the first period when his screen shot found its way past Rinne, who complained, to no avail, that he was interfered with. Nashville responded before the end of the period, though, when Joel Ward got his own rebound and beat Roberto Luongo with a quick shot.

The Canucks took control in the second period, scoring the only goal and playing with the poise of a team in control. Alexander Edler beat Rinne with another screen shot at 9:43, but later in the period the Predators had a two-man advantage for forty-seven seconds and couldn't score. This was a situation that pitted the will and determination of the teams against

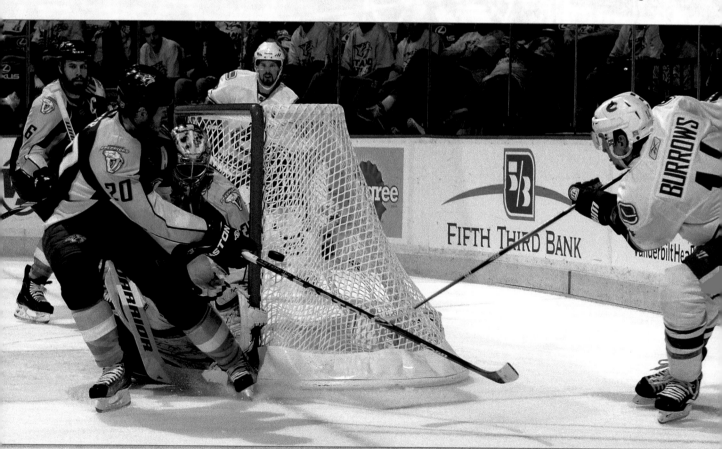

Alexandre Burrows cleverly lifts the puck in front, hoping to bank it in off goalie Pekka Rinne who is tight to the near post.

Nashville's Mike Fisher re-directs a cross-ice pass towards the Vancouver net, but he misses the open side.

Conference Semi-Final — Vancouver Canucks vs. Nashville Predators

Despite being well checked, Nashville's Joel Ward manages to get a shot past goalie Roberto Luongo in the first period.

each other, and Vancouver came out on the winning side at a time the game might well have been decided.

"It was a big turning point," Vancouver coach Alain Vigneault acknowledged. "They used their timeout. They were in striking distance and we got a couple big plays from our goaltender and we got a great job from Dan Hamhuis, Alex Burrows, and Ryan Kesler, who were out there for almost the full five-on-three doing the right things."

Still, the Predators tied the game early in the third period when Cody Franson scored on another screen shot that Luongo didn't have much of a chance on. But Vancouver was not going to be forced into another overtime thanks to the bullish Kesler.

First, he drew Ryan Suter into a hooking penalty at 6:21 of the third to gain a power play for the Canucks. Then, he did it all to score the go-ahead goal a minute later. Charging through the middle, he split the top defensive pairing of Shea Weber and Shane O'Brien and then ripped a high shot to the stick side of Rinne for one of the best goals of the playoffs.

The Predators pulled Rinne in the final minute, resulting in an empty-net goal from the struggling Henrik Sedin. Vancouver was now heading home with a chance to end the series and gain some valuable rest days over the remaining teams left in the chase for the Stanley Cup.

GAME FIVE — *May 7, 2011*

Nashville 4 at Vancouver 3

(Vancouver leads series 3–2)

The Canucks had a chance to close out the series on home ice, but they were only the second-best team at Rogers Arena this night, losing to a more desperate and determined Nashville team by a 4–3 score. Joel Ward, who had just ten goals in the regular season, scored two goals, including his league-leading seventh of the playoffs, to get the win. David Legwand also scored twice for the Predators.

"Our backs were against the wall, so we talked about one game and we're going to talk about one game again," Nashville coach Barry Trotz said. "It was a great character test for everybody. This team is exactly what I told you. They are resilient and a great group to work with day in and day out. We are not perfect, but we do come to play."

And tonight, with a long summer staring them in the eyes, the team responded with a great win.

Just as Vancouver had done on the road the previous game, Nashville scored an early goal to worry the crowd. Legwand did the damage at 3:42, short-handed no less, a mere eleven seconds after Sergei Kostitsyn had taken a penalty for holding the stick. But half a minute after Kostitsyn came out of the box, Raffi Torres tied the game with his first goal of the playoffs to get the jitters out of the way.

By the end of the period, it seemed the Canucks were in control. Kesler got his fourth goal in the last three games at 15:06 to give the Canucks the lead, but Legwand tied the game in the first minute of the second period. That was all the scoring through forty minutes, and the Canucks were in good position to win and then rest.

But Ward came out in the third and took control. He scored the go-ahead goal just seventy-four

Mason Raymond races up ice as teammates watch and a Nashville player gives chase.

Conference Semi-Final — Vancouver Canucks vs. Nashville Predators

53

Ryan Kesler goes hard to the net and is rewarded when he gets his stick on the puck and deflects it in.

seconds into the period thanks to a great play from Mike Fisher. He stopped a clearing from Kevin Bieksa near the faceoff circle to Luongo's left and wound up for a big shot. Instead, though, he fired the puck to the other side where Ward one-timed a bullet shot past a surprised Luongo who couldn't make the adjustment in time.

Ward got the insurance goal in a similar way. This time Jordin Tootoo took advantage of a Vancouver turnover, and instead of shooting found Ward to the back side of the goal where he had only to snap a shot into the open side.

"He's been great this series. He's been our best player in this series," Rinne said of the hot Ward. "It's great to see. He works hard. He is just a great team guy and typical kind of Predators' player. He's getting rewarded for being a tough guy to play against.

He always plays against the top lines and now he's contributing offensively."

It was only then that Vancouver played with a determination it should have started the game with, peppering Rinne with shots in the closing minutes but unable to beat the Finnish goalie who was his usual unflappable self. Ryan Kesler got one goal back at 16:14, but it was too little, too late. A series once under control was now headed back to enemy territory for game six, and Vancouver's grasp was more tenuous than it had been a day ago. And while Kesler was playing sensational hockey, the Sedins had been all but invisible in the series, something that had to change if the Canucks were going to go deep in the playoffs.

"I didn't want us to play on our heels," Trotz revealed. "If we are going to get back in the series, let's go for it. Let's go for it. Our guys responded."

Henrik Sedin (left) and Kevin Klein chase a loose puck into the corner.

Conference Semi-Final — Vancouver Canucks vs. Nashville Predators

55

GAME SIX — *May 9, 2011*

Vancouver 3 at Nashville 1
*(**Vancouver** wins series 4–2)*

The Canucks advanced to the Conference final thanks to two goals in the first period and some exceptional defensive play over the final fifty minutes of the game. The win was an exclamation point for Ryan Kesler who assisted on both goals and had a hand in eleven of his team's fourteen goals in the series.

"He just had one of those series that is absolutely remarkable for one player," Nashville coach Barry Trotz said in frustrated admiration. "I thought—as I said as I was going by him [shaking hands]—if he doesn't play that way, we're probably going to game seven and we might win the series. He played to a level that few people can reach."

Indeed, Kesler had forty-one goals in the regular season, a career high, and he was turning 2010–11 into a career-defining moment in which a star became a superstar, a game changer capable of taking the team on his back. And with the Sedins struggling, his higher level of play couldn't have come at a better time.

On the first goal of the game, at 7:45 of the first, Kesler dumped the puck in and chased after it. Nashville defenceman Ryan Suter got to it first, but Kesler stole it and backhanded the puck into the slot in one motion. Mason Raymond was there to take the pass, and his quick deke beat Pekka Rinne for a 1–0 lead.

Less than two minutes later, on the power play, Kesler was the in-between player from Henrik to Daniel Sedin, the latter finishing the play with a shot that beat Rinne clearly. The two-goal lead was the first in the series for the Canucks, excepting their empty-netter at the end of game four.

Goalie Roberto Luongo allowed the Predators some life in the second period. David Legwand scored from nearly the goal line on a terrible play from the goalie, and the Preds buzzed around the rest of the

Christian Ehrhoff (left) checks Joel Ward as the two meet in the corner.

56

Conference Semi-Final — Vancouver Canucks vs. Nashville Predators

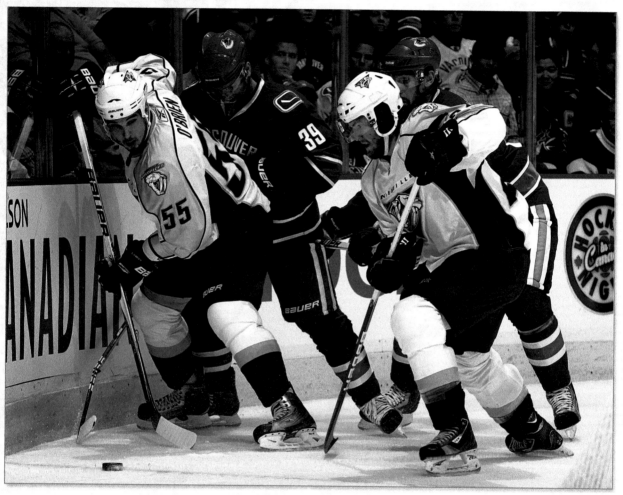

Shane O'Brien shields the puck along the boards looking for help or a way to fend off his check.

period, limiting the Canucks to just two shots in the middle period. Luongo atoned for his gaffe, though, by coming up big when he had to.

He also had a bit of luck. Mike Fisher shot wide on a great set-up from Martin Erat on a two-on-one, and later in the period Erat had a breakaway but was caught by the speedy Jeff Tambellini, who prevented Erat from even getting shot away.

The key to victory was the third period, though. Teams only all too often see a 2–1 lead and automatically nurse it, trying desperately to hold on while allowing the opposition to gain the puck in the offensive end. But the Canucks started their defensive strategy in the Nashville end, forechecking hard and containing the Predators as they tried to break out of their own end. The result was a 10–6 shots advantage in the third and very few scoring chances.

"I thought that was our best period of the series," opined Daniel Sedin. "We didn't give them anything. That's how we need to play as a team and when we do that we're successful."

Kesler echoed those sentiments. "We took it to them rather than sitting back," he said. "That was the theme going into the third. We didn't want to sit back and hope. We wanted to take it to them, get shots on net, throw everything we had at them, empty the tanks. We did it and that was our best period of the series."

The win also gave the Canucks a bit of extra time off as San Jose and Detroit were still battling in the other conference semi-final. When asked which team he'd prefer to face, Vancouver coach Alain Vigneault said: "We're not in this to just win one round, and we're not in this to just win two rounds."

Conference Semi-Final — Vancouver Canucks vs. Nashville Predators

57

After the battle, goalies Pekka Rinne (left) and Roberto Luongo share a congratulatory smile.

GAME ONE — *May 15, 2011*

San Jose 2 at **Vancouver 3**

(Vancouver leads series 1-0)

The opening game of the series featured two distinct parts thanks to results of the teams' previous games. Vancouver beat Nashville in six games and hadn't played in six days while the Sharks beat Detroit in seven and had three days to recover. The result was a fast start from San Jose while the Canucks looked out of playoff shape and then came a dominant final twenty-five minutes by the home side as the visitors faded badly.

The Sharks had leads of 1–0 and 2–1, but two quick goals and far more energy by Vancouver in the third gave the team its third successive win to start a series.

"I just think we finally found our legs," Vancouver forward Ryan Kesler suggested. "We were a little rusty in the first period. I thought we played well, but I think second and third period we found that extra gear and we continued. We forced them and we put a lot of pucks on the net. We generated most of the offense."

Sharks coach Todd McLellan was in full agreement. "We were like dogs chasing cars down the freeway," he noted with metaphoric flavour. "We weren't catching anybody. We put the puck into very poor spots. They eventually beat us at the type of game we want to play. We tried to put on a brave face and we talked about being fresh and mentally ready to go. I thought for thirty-seven minutes we were able to skate. Basically what happened, I thought the team that potentially was rusty, because they hadn't played for a while, found their legs while we lost ours. When you look at the route we took to get here, they had a few days off and we had an emotional, taxing game. We're lucky enough to be playing, but we've got get better."

Joe Thornton got the only goal of the opening period after a bad giveaway by goalie Roberto Luongo gave

San Jose goalie Antti Niemi and Mason Raymond look high for the puck while Kent Huskins tries to check Raymond.

Conference Final — Vancouver Canucks vs. San Jose Sharks

59

Alexander Edler collides with Dany Heatley as they both go after the puck.

Conference Final — Vancouver Canucks vs. San Jose Sharks

him a freebie. The goal came at 18:47 and sucked the life out of the Canucks as they headed to the dressing room for the first intermission, but they regrouped and tied the score early in the second when Maxim Lapierre got his first goal of the 2011 playoffs.

Midway through the period, the Sharks regained the lead off a Patrick Marleau goal on the power play, but with about five minutes left in the second the tide turned and the Canucks found a new gear that San Jose couldn't match. Sharks goalie Antti Niemi had to be particularly sharp late in the period, making highlight-reel saves off Ryan Kesler and Jannik Hansen to keep his team in the lead, but the Canucks continued to dominate in the third and were rewarded.

Kevin Bieksa tied the game at 7:02 of the third when he wired a high shot over Niemi's glove, and just seventy-nine seconds later Henrik Sedin got the go-ahead goal on the power play, controlling a nice pass from Christian Ehrhoff at the point and backhanding the puck over Niemi. It was his first goal of the playoffs that wasn't an empty netter and helped quell the growing criticism for his excellent regular season and poor showing so far in the playoffs (9 points, and, more worrisome, a minus-8 rating in the first 13 games).

Once the Canucks went ahead, though, they continued to pour on the pressure, never giving the tired-looking Sharks a chance to get back into the game. Said coach Alain Vigneault: "I thought the last twenty-five minutes we played our best hockey of the game. We went north-south real quickly. We made their defencemen turn back and go for pucks, and we were able to create turnovers off of that that led to time in their end, good quality time."

The Canucks knew they had some good fortune on their side in the victory, though, and knew any fatigue the Sharks felt would be gone by the time game two which would be played after a three-day break.

Mikael Samuelsson races up ice with a little bit of room ahead.

GAME TWO — *May 18, 2011*

San Jose 3 at **Vancouver 7**

(Vancouver leads series 2–0)

By the end of the night, it was hard to believe San Jose led 1–0 in this game or that the score was tied 2–2 after twenty minutes. By the end of the night, the Canucks were so much the dominant team that many Sharks players called their effort embarrassing.

"It's embarrassing," said San Jose's Logan Couture. "That's the only word that comes to mind. We're in the conference finals, in the Stanley Cup playoffs, and to put an effort out like that—I feel bad for the fans and for the coaching staff that we gave an effort like that tonight."

For Vancouver fans, though, the game was a relief because the Sedin twins brought their A game and were their old, game-leading selves. Daniel Sedin had two power-play goals, while Henrik had three assists, and the Canucks took a close game and blew it open in the final period, one marred by bad blood with only nine seconds left on the clock.

Logan Couture got the first goal just 2:28 into the game on a Sharks power play, but midway through the period Vancouver scored twice in thirty-nine seconds to take the lead. Daniel scored with the extra man and soon after Raffi Torres made it 2–1, but Patrick Marleau tied the game with Daniel in the penalty box for cross-checking.

Marc-Edouard Vlasic snaps a one-timer while goalie Roberto Luongo goes down and spreads the trapper across the front of the goal.

Raffi Torres raises his arms after a goal while Antti Niemi sits disconsolately in his crease and Marc-Edouard Vlasic looks on helplessly.

Douglas Murray fends off Chris Higgins as he goes behind his net looking for the puck.

Kevin Bieksa got the only goal of the middle period for Vancouver, but that 3–2 lead only widened in the third as the Sharks simply lost focus. Key to their troubles was the play of Ben Eager. He took a roughing minor in the first and a boarding penalty in the second after trying to put Daniel through the boards, but in the third he lost all control or sense of team commitment, taking three more minors and a misconduct before being escorted off the ice at 19:51.

The Canucks, meanwhile, scored four goals in a row to make it a 7–2 game, the first coming with Eager in the box and the second with Devin Setoguchi serving a too-many-men penalty. Chris Higgins and Daniel Sedin got those goals, and then Aaron Rome and Mason Raymond put the game out of reach.

Eager scored at 17:27 to close out the scoring when he knocked in a pass right on the doorstep of goalie Roberto Luongo. As the play ended, the net came off and Luongo fell inside, and Eager stood over the prone goalie taunting him, earning another minor for his efforts. All players congregated on the ice in the dying seconds, so referees Dan O'Halloran and Tim Peel simply handed out four misconducts to get the disturbers off.

"We've talked about playing whistle to whistle, staying disciplined," said Vancouver coach Alain Vigneault. "That's what we've done throughout the playoffs. We did it again tonight. When their fourth-line player took a run at the NHL leading scorer, possibly the MVP, we stayed focused, we stayed disciplined. You know, we went out and played."

GAME THREE — *May 20, 2011*

Vancouver 3 at **San Jose** 4

(Vancouver leads series 2–1)

This was as important a game as any in the franchise history of San Jose. Trailing 2–0 in the series, a loss would have virtually guaranteed a Vancouver win and trip to the Stanley Cup Final for the Canucks, and the Sharks would once again be the focus of another great regular season followed by a too-short playoff run. With the core of the team in its prime, this was a team built to win right now, but in the last six years the Sharks always fell short in the third round of the playoffs—when they made it that far.

One of those veterans, Joe Thornton, led the team to victory with three assists and some dominating play. That brought his playoff total to seventeen points, tops in the league. Even still, it was a game they almost lost control of late in the third period.

But first, the Canucks couldn't match the desperation of San Jose in the critical first period, falling behind 3–0 after twenty minutes and, ultimately, never quite able to recover. One of Thornton's linemates, Patrick Marleau, got the first and third goals. The first, at 3:56, on the power play by taking a pass from Thornton behind the goal, and the third on a clear breakaway after a great pass again from Thornton. Marleau snapped a shot over the outstretched glove of Roberto Luongo, and the game was pretty much over. Sort of.

"Obviously they wanted to come out hard in front of their fans," Luongo said. "We talked about making

Devin Setoguchi goes one-on-one against Roberto Luongo, the goalie getting the upper hand on this drive.

Ryan Kesler collides with Douglas Murray.

Conference Final — Vancouver Canucks vs. San Jose Sharks

San Jose's Dany Heatley lets go a slapshot while Tanner Glass does what he can to get in the way.

sure we make the good plays in the first ten minutes, playing hard and not giving them anything. But obviously they generated stuff off the power play."

The Sharks played solid hockey in the middle period but ran into penalty trouble that could have been costly. Twice they gave Vancouver five-on-three power play advantages, but goalie Antti Niemi was perfect when he had to be and didn't allow the visitors to generate any momentum.

Even when Alexandre Burrows cut the lead to two goals early in the third, the Sharks didn't panic. Dan Boyle responded soon after with another power-play marker at 6:46, but then Jamie McGinn gave Vancouver something to work with. He crushed Aaron Rome into the boards from behind and earned a five-minute

major and game misconduct, and just like that the Canucks woke up.

Henrik Sedin fed defenceman Dan Hamhuis a perfect pass which Hamhuis drilled home on a one-timer to make it 4–2 at 13:39, and later on the long power play, Kevin Bieksa scored on a deflected shot to make it a one-goal game.

With Luongo on the bench and the Canucks pressing, the game was tense, but in the end the Sharks held them at bay and won the game to get right back into the series. But as Thornton noted, "Every game for us right now is game seven. We realize how important tonight was. Next game is just going to be more important. We realize what's at stake."

Conference Final — Vancouver Canucks vs. San Jose Sharks

67

GAME FOUR — *May 20, 2011*
Vancouver 4 at San Jose 2
(Vancouver leads series 3–1)

In one of the strangest playoff periods you'll ever see, the Vancouver Canucks scored three five-on-three power-play goals in a span of just 1:55 midway through the second period to carry them to a crucial victory and a chance to eliminate San Jose at home two days later.

Henrik Sedin had four assists and brother Daniel had three, but it was two goals by Sami Salo in that second period that made the biggest impact. For the Sharks, the real prospect of not making it to the Stanley Cup Final yet again was difficult to grasp—but all too real by game's end.

The first period was scoreless as both teams knew the implication of the game. A San Jose win means the series is tied 2–2, but a Vancouver win makes it all but impossible for the Sharks to recover. Yet San Jose had the early advantage. It had the only three power plays in the opening period and had the first two chances in the second as well, but all five opportunities went for naught, giving the Canucks a psychological advantage and moral boost.

And then a strange series of penalties occurred against the Sharks, as one might expect. First, Dany Heatley took an undisciplined penalty for high sticking

A scrum jams the crease as players fight for the puck which squirts harmlessly away from the Vancouver goal.

Keith Ballard sends Jamie McGinn flying with an old-style hip check along the boards.

Conference Final — Vancouver Canucks vs. San Jose Sharks

69

at 8:15, and just fifty seconds later Torrey Mitchell was whistled for hooking. On the ensuing five-on-three, Ryan Kesler drilled a hard shot past Niemi at 9:16.

But at 10:39, the Sharks were called for too many men, and this time Salo set up in the middle of the ice and blew a shot past Niemi on a second five-on-three just sixteen seconds later. Then, since both good and bad things come in threes, Douglas Murray cleared the puck over the glass and got two minutes for delay of game, and ten seconds later, Salo blew another hard shot in to make it 3–0.

Of course any time a team has three five-on-threes against it, it looks to the referees to blame, but this was all self-inflicted. There wasn't anything debatable about any of the four quick penalties that sunk the Sharks.

Henrik Sedin made the play of the game early in the third period. Charging down the right wing on a two-on-one with Alexandre Burrows, he seemed to run out of options and space for a pass and didn't have a good angle to shoot. But he came in on goal and Niemi played the shot only to see Henrik slide a pass between the goalie's legs, through the crease, and onto the waiting stick of Burrows, who had only to re-direct the puck into the open net.

"Every time I have a chance to go on a two-on-one with him, I just keep my stick on the ice," Burrows said. "That one, I barely saw it come through. It just hit my blade and went in."

The Sharks came back with a pair of goals, but the Canucks played with a poise that never suggested a collapse was in the cards. With about ten minutes left in the game, Raffi Torres hit Joe Thornton hard, and Thornton left the ice and didn't come back. He played in game five but was ineffective. The Canucks won this game on the power play—and in the alley—and were going home with a chance to close the series out.

Henrik Sedin celebrates a goal after Alexandre Burrows converted his perfect pass.

GAME FIVE — *May 24, 2011*

San Jose 2 at **Vancouver 3**

*(**Vancouver** wins series 4–1)*

It was a strange game and an even stranger goal that ended the series, but when both teams left the Rogers Arena at the end of the night, Vancouver was heading to the Stanley Cup Final and the Sharks were heading to another summer of "what if…?" and "what happened?"

Kevin Bieksa scored at 10:18 of the second overtime to give the Canucks the win—and a week's rest—but Ryan Kesler was another hero and Roberto Luongo a third. And, in truth, the better team didn't win this night. The Sharks were dominant and in control most of the night, but one small lapse in concentration did them in.

Alexandre Burrows got the only goal of the first period at 8:02, but the team played as if the game were over with that one score. Inevitably, San Jose tied the game, midway through the second, when Dan Boyle's power-play shot beat Luongo, and just twenty-four seconds into the final period Devin Setoguchi put the Sharks ahead after taking a sensational pass from Joe Pavelski.

The Canucks looked thoroughly defeated and showed little energy, and the fans were likewise unemotional at such a critical time in the series. The Canucks had lost game five in both previous playoff rounds and seemed destined to lose for a third time.

But as the clock wound down, Luongo headed to the bench for a sixth attacker, and Ryan Kesler got a piece of Daniel Sedin's quick shot, fooling Antti Niemi

Keith Ballard takes off up ice as Jamal Mayers of San Jose tries to track him down.

Conference Final — Vancouver Canucks vs. San Jose Sharks

71

and forcing overtime. In the fourth period, the Sharks dominated, but they couldn't beat the unflappable Luongo.

"We had tons of chances. We had about five, six, or seven shifts where we were in their end and we just threw everything at them," Sharks defenceman Dan Boyle admitted. "We missed a lot of freaking chances, but that's the name of the game—you've got to bury them. Obviously we have to give Lu credit, but that's on us. I think we had the chances, the looks, and didn't put it in."

Midway through the second OT, Bieksa scored what can only be described as a phantom goal. Vancouver had control of the puck inside the San Jose blue-line. Alexander Edler, at the right point, merely kept the puck in by firing it around the glass, a play you'll see a hundred times a game. But the

puck hit a stanchion holding the sheets of glass together and bounced back to the point where Bieksa was stationed. Quite literally, he was the only player who saw the puck. Sharks players raised their hands to indicate the puck had gone into the mesh. Goalie Niemi went behind his net and then back to his crease, realizing it wasn't coming to him. Canucks players stopped skating.

But Bieksa took a quick shot that wobbled and bobbled into the low corner of the net while Niemi stared ahead blankly. The red goal light came on, and then everyone realized the game was over.

"I just one-timed it on net and not many people knew where it was," Bieksa said. "It was just a knuckleball. I barely got enough on it to put it on net. It was a hard puck to shoot. It was probably the ugliest goal of my career, but the biggest."

Captain Henrik Sedin decided to pose with—but not lift—the Clarence Campbell Bowl after the presentation by Deputy Commissioner Bill Daly.

"The only guy that knew where the puck was Kevin Bieksa," San Jose coach Todd McLellan said. "When you watch the replay, the officials didn't know where it was, Nemo [Niemi] didn't know where it was, Vancouver, San Jose, nobody knew where it was. It came right to Bieksa. One more bounce, he probably whiffs on it, we're still playing."

Offered Niemi: "I saw the puck bounce, then I didn't see it. I looked back and looked in front, and then it came." Too late.

More luckily for the Canucks, no official blew his whistle to stop play. In the end, Kesler saved the day, then Luongo, and, finally, Bieksa. For the first time since 1994, the Canucks were going to play for the Stanley Cup.

Always a special moment, this handshake line sees Henrik Sedin congratulate Dany Heatley of the losing Sharks.

Conference Final — Vancouver Canucks vs. San Jose Sharks

73

GAME ONE — *June 1, 2011*

Boston 0 at **Vancouver 1**
(Vancouver leads series 1-0)

For the third time in four playoff series, the Vancouver Canucks started with a win courtesy of a shutout from Roberto Luongo, and for the fourth time, they started with a win. The hero tonight was Raffi Torres, who scored a dramatic goal with just 18.5 seconds left in regulation time, the game's only goal. It came thanks to three sensational plays in a matter of seconds.

First, Ryan Kesler beat Johnny Boychuk to the puck at the Boston blue-line, got the puck over the line and stayed onside. Then, he fired a cross-ice pass to winger Jannik Hansen, who had moved in on the play. Hansen then waited until big defenceman Zdeno Chara fell to the ice trying to block either a pass or shot, managing to get the puck to Torres streaking to the goal.

Torres then got his stick down and re-directed the hard pass beyond the reach of goalie Tim Thomas, who had been the best player for either side all night. A sloppy but thrilling opening game ended with a victory for the Canucks, and two of the goalies nominated for the Vezina Trophy were their team's best players all night.

"He [Hansen] got himself into a position where I started respecting the shot and started to cut down

Vancouver's Ryan Kesler and Boston's giant captain Zdeno Chara go toe-to-toe in front of the Bruins goal.

the angle," Thomas described. "He was able to pass it to the guy (Torres) who was cutting to the net, who I didn't even see was there."

Hansen had been stoned five minutes into the third period by Thomas on a clear breakaway as he chose to put the puck between the goalie's legs only to have Thomas get down low and make the critical save.

The game could be divided into two distinct parts—the first two periods and the third period. In the first part, teams exchanged a seemingly countless number of penalties, yet neither side could score. For Boston, the power play drought continued as it went 0–for–6, that part of the game being the team's weakest all playoffs. But for the Canucks, the man advantage had

Daniel Sedin leaps out of the way as goalie Tim Thomas makes a save.

Stanley Cup Final — Vancouver Canucks vs. Boston Bruins

75

Raffi Torres re-directs a perfect pass from Jannik Hansen with just 18.5 seconds left in regulation to give the Canucks a 1-0 win.

been a sizeable bonus for eighteen games, so their inability to score was surprising.

In the third period, though, the referees put away their whistles and didn't call a single minor after signaling thirteen in the first forty minutes. And the Canucks dominated play, time and again, creating great chances but just unable to beat Thomas, who sparkled in the Boston cage. It seemed only a matter of time before they would score, but as the clock sped towards 0:00, it also looked more certain that the game would go to overtime. And then Kesler started the game-deciding play.

"Obviously, in the third period they were the better team, and they ended up scoring that goal," admitted Boston coach Claude Julien. "It got away from us, but we still got an opportunity here in the next game to hopefully get that one and kind of get the home-ice advantage."

At the other end, Luongo was equally reliable when needed, and as the game went on it became clear the first goal wouldn't just be a big goal—it would likely be the game winner. Incredibly, though, Luongo had now won the first game of the last eight playoff series in which he played.

76

Stanley Cup Final — Vancouver Canucks vs. Boston Bruins

GAME TWO — *June 4, 2011*

Boston 2 at **Vancouver 3**

(Vancouver leads series 2-0)

Alexandre Burrows capped a career night by scoring just eleven seconds into the first overtime period to give the Canucks a 3–2, come-from-behind win and take a controlling 2–0 lead in the Stanley Cup Final. Burrows also opened the scoring in the first and assisted on Daniel Sedin's tying goal midway through the third which produced the overtime.

It was his third OT winner in 2011 and came close to the all-time record for fastest overtime goal, set by Montreal's Brian Skrudland in 1986 against Calgary. The goal put Burrows in rare and exclusive company, for only Mel Hill in 1939 and Maurice Richard in 1951 have scored three extra-time winners in one playoff year (Hill got all of his in one series, no less).

It was a game that at times was strategically defensive and at other times wide open as teams exchanged glorious scoring chances. As in game one, the goalies were as much of the story as any of the skaters, but tonight it was the gambling style of Boston's Tim Thomas that cost the team a win. On the winning goal, Burrows skated down the left wing, faked a shot to draw Thomas way out of the net, and then wrapped the puck around and in from the far side. Thomas, known to come well out to challenge shooters, lost out on this play, but it's a style that has worked well for him throughout his renaissance.

"I know Tim Thomas likes to challenge," Burrows explained. "If I shoot there, I think he stops it. So I wanted to walk around and shoot it right away but he tripped me and I lost the puck a little bit. I was lucky enough just to be able to wrap it."

The Bruins had the same lineup as game one, but Vancouver coach Alain Vigneault made two changes. First, he inserted Andrew Alberts for Dan Hamhuis, who was injured in the series opener, and then he

Goalie Roberto Luongo makes a pad save while Milan Lucic tries to cause a distraction in front.

Stanley Cup Final — Vancouver Canucks vs. Boston Bruins

77

Alexandre Burrows starts the play that leads to the OT winner, faking goalie Tim Thomas and going behind the net.

gave Manny Malhotra his first start since mid-March when Malhotra suffered a serious eye injury.

Burrows got the only goal of the first period on a power play after Zdeno Chara was called for interference on Ryan Kesler. It was his eighth goal of the playoffs but first with the extra man, and it came on a quick shot that Thomas wasn't expecting. The play was set up thanks to a beautiful touch pass from Chris Higgins, and Burrows's shot snuck under the blocker arm of Thomas.

Boston, sensing the urgency of the game, came out and played its best period of the series in the second, scoring twice and dominating play. Milan Lucic tied the game on a Boston power play, sliding a rebound under Luongo, and then Mark Recchi scored a beautiful goal when he redirected a quick Chara point shot while drifting through the slot.

But the Canucks took the play to Boston in the third while the Bruins tried to nurse the lead. Thomas had to make several good saves, but time and again he came out well beyond the blue ice to cut down the angle. This proved costly on the tying goal. A quick point shot from Alexander Edler was deflected by Daniel Sedin in front, but it ended up on Burrows's stick. He dished the puck off to Sedin again, and while Thomas was splayed out on the ice five feet from his goal line, Sedin snapped the puck in the empty net.

"I think that comes from him knowing where we're going to be and we know where he's going to be," said Henrik Sedin of Burrows. "In those areas, he looks up and knows Danny is going to come there. That comes from playing together for a long time. He made a great play there."

That set the stage for Burrows's incredibly quick OT winner, propelling Vancouver into a commanding lead in the series. It was Boston's first overtime loss this playoffs after four straight wins while the Canucks improved to 4–2. As well, Boston had been 6–0 when leading after forty minutes, but that perfect record, too, now had a blemish thanks to Burrows.

Great as Vancouver's start to the series had been, though, Burrows cautioned against over-enthusiasm. "We haven't won anything yet," he noted. "It's only two games. We've only taken care of home ice. They're a really good team and I'm sure they're going to feed off the energy from their crowd. We have to make sure we're ready to go in there. It won't be easy. Until you win a road game, you're not in control of any series."

Burrows and Henrik Sedin celebrate. (insert) Burrows completes his winning play by lunging for the puck and swiping it into the net just eleven seconds into overtime.

Stanley Cup Final — Vancouver Canucks vs. Boston Bruins

79

GAME THREE — *June 6, 2011*

Vancouver 1 at **Boston 8**
(Vancouver leads series 2-1)

Well, no one predicted a sweep, and a sweep was not in the cards after the Bruins opened a huge lead in the second period and rolled to a one-sided win in game three. It was, in truth, a must-win game for the Bruins because to have lost would have meant being 3–0 down in the series. Only once in Stanley Cup Final history has a team overcome such a deficit to win, and that was in 1942 (Toronto).

"This team has done that in the past when it was tested and I think we did it again tonight, "said Andrew Ference. "It wasn't pretty. It was Boston hockey."

The victory was fuelled by, of all things, special teams, that part of the game that had been the Bruins' greatest nemesis all playoffs long. More to the point, the Bruins scored two power-play goals and two short-handed goals, taking a scoreless game after twenty minutes and turning it into a rout by the end of the second period.

But perhaps the most important moment in the game came early in the first period. Boston's Nathan

Vancouver's Chris Higgins is stopped point blank by Tim Thomas while defenceman Zdeno Chara looks on.

80

Stanley Cup Final — Vancouver Canucks vs. Boston Bruins

Henrik Sedin goes to the net only to be checked by goalie Tim Thomas who plays the body and ignores the puck.

Horton was the victim of a head shot from Aaron Rome after making a pass just inside the Vancouver blue-line. Rome was given a five-minute major for interference and a game misconduct, and Horton was carried off on a stretcher. Boston didn't capitalize on the long power play, and Horton, of course, didn't return for the rest of the game, but the Bruins drew inspiration from the play and took it to the Canucks in the second period.

"It is so tough when you see a guy go down like that," said Brad Marchand. "You are so worried about him. We're all so close in this room and we care about Horty a lot. It played on our mind in the rest of the first period, but we were able to use it to our advantage after that."

Just as eleven seconds was huge in game two, the time that Alexandre Burrows scored in overtime to give Vancouver a 3–2 win, so, too, was it big this night. Just eleven seconds into the second period Andrew Ference blew a slapshot past Roberto Luongo to give the home side a 1–0 lead, a lead they never relinquished. Four minutes later, forty-three-year-old Mark Recchi scored on the power play, although this time he merely got credit for a goal redirected accidentally by Vancouver's Ryan Kesler past Luongo.

The killer came midway through the period when Marchand converted a short-handed chance. He beat the Vancouver defence on a rush, and as he slid across the crease and outwaited the falling, sprawling

Stanley Cup Final — Vancouver Canucks vs. Boston Bruins

81

Boston's David Krejci celebrates his second-period goal to give his team a commanding 4–0 lead.

Luongo he roofed a shot to make it 3–0, more or less sealing the victory in the process. David Krejci scored his eleventh playoff goal late in the period to make it 4–0, and in the third Tim Thomas held the fort as Vancouver tried in vain to get back into the game.

"All of a sudden, it was like the wheels fell off a bit and everything was going their way," offered Luongo. "You know, obviously, it's one of those games where we are all disappointed with the result. But, at the end of the day, a loss is a loss."

Daniel Paille got the second short-handed goal of the game midway through the final period when his shot squirted under the glove arm of Luongo, and Jannik Hansen's goal merely ended Thomas's shutout. Boston tallied three late goals in a game in which everything and anything it put on net went in.

For Boston, it had to keep this fortuitous scoring going another game, and for the Canucks, they had to erase this result from their memory. After all, a win in game four would allow them to go home and win the Cup two nights later at their own Rogers Arena. A loss would tie the series and make the outcome of the Stanley Cup Final entirely up in the air.

GAME FOUR — *June 8, 2011*

Vancouver 0 at **Boston 4**

(series tied 2–2)

The Boston Bruins finished their mini home stand by doing exactly what Vancouver had done—winning the two games on their own ice. They did so with another emphatic victory, making for an interesting lead-up to game five. Vancouver had home-ice advantage still in what was now a best-of-three series, but the Bruins had all the momentum.

Again it was a massive second period that proved the difference as they took a 1–0 lead after twenty minutes and turned it into a game-winning 3–0 lead. They added a goal early in the third, which forced Vancouver coach Alain Vigneault to pull goalie Roberto Luongo and give Cory Schneider his first taste of Stanley Cup Final play.

While the Bruins continued to be inspired by the injury to Nathan Horton, the Sedins continued to play on the periphery, unwilling to go hard to the net or play a physical game. The result was an ineffective offence that was stifled further by the flawless play of Tim Thomas in the Boston goal.

There were three lineup changes tonight. For Vancouver, Aaron Rome was out with his series-ending suspension, and in his place was Keith Ballard. As well, Jeff Tambellini was a healthy scratch and Tanner Glass was inserted for the first time in the Stanley Cup

Rich Peverley celebrates his first-period goal which got the Bruins off and running to victory.

Stanley Cup Final — Vancouver Canucks vs. Boston Bruins

83

Peverley beats Roberto Luongo by sliding the puck through the goalie's pads on a breakaway.

Final. And for Boston, rookie sensation Tyler Seguin was in the lineup to replace Horton.

The Bruins got the only goal of the first period thanks to a great play by David Krejci at the Vancouver blue-line. He dove to poke the puck free, and Rich Peverley went in alone on goal, beating Luongo with a goal through the pads at 11:59. That was all the Bruins needed to swing the momentum in their favour this night. Vancouver simply couldn't match the intensity or pace the Bruins came at their opponents with, and that slim lead never seemed in danger.

In the second, the two Boston goals came in a two-minute stretch in the middle part of the period. Michael Ryder took a routine shot from the top of the circle which may or may not have been tipped by defenceman Sami Salo, but it eluded Luongo even though the goalie should have had the shot.

Brad Marchand made it 3–0 on a great play from Patrice Bergeron. He went in behind the Vancouver net to get the puck, and Henrik Sedin wanted nothing to do with a bodycheck and moved out of the way, losing the puck and the angle to the goal at the same time. Bergeron got the puck out front and Marchand back-handed it over the big glove of Luongo.

Peverley added his second of the night at 3:39 of the third, and that was the game. Vancouver now had to find a way to stem the incredible tide that was the Bruins' confidence, and it had to be prepared to "get dirty" in the tough areas of the ice if it were going to have any chance to use home ice to its advantage.

Said Thomas: "Every time this year that we've faced adversity as a team, we've rose to the challenge. We needed to do it one more time because we were down 2–0. Now we've done that for two games. The challenge for us will be to keep doing that."

The Bruins got a further lift when Horton, released from hospital only the previous day with a serious concussion, visited his teammates in the dressing room after the victory.

"I was very, very happy to see Nathan up and around in the locker room," Thomas said. "I wasn't exactly sure of his status."

"It's 2–2 and that's the way you look at it," said beleaguered Vancouver defenceman Kevin Bieksa. "They won their two at home and we won our two, so it looks like it could be a homer series and luckily we have two of the next three at home."

The Bruins faced two must-win games at home and won, and now Vancouver faced a must-win game. To lose game five would mean going to Boston with the Stanley Cup in the building and the Bruins ready to win.

84

Stanley Cup Final — Vancouver Canucks vs. Boston Bruins

Jubilant Bruins in front and disconsolate goalie Roberto Luongo in back. That was the story for game four.

Stanley Cup Final — Vancouver Canucks vs. Boston Bruins

85

GAME FIVE — *June 10, 2011*

Boston 0 at **Vancouver 1**

(Vancouver leads series 3-2)

After five games, this series could now clearly be divided into two—Vancouver home games, all won by the home team with dramatic and late goals, and Boston games which were two lop-sided victories, also by the home side. More particularly, it might be divided into games in which the goalies did, or didn't do, their thing.

Vancouver goalie Roberto Luongo was sensational at home, and he struggled on the road. More interestingly, Tim Thomas was incredible in all games, but in the three Vancouver wins he allowed a decisive goal in each as a result of his aggressive style of play.

Tonight, Luongo stopped all 31 shots he faced, while Thomas was one shy of perfection, stopping 24 of 25.

Perhaps most impressively for the Canucks, they played a sensational defensive game, generated some good scoring chances, and won a close game after being hammered in Beantown in games three and four.

"It's the Stanley Cup Final, nobody said it was going to be easy," Maxim Lapierre said. "We just had to regroup and bounce back, and this is what we did. We were patient with the game plan, and we got our break."

In game five, the hero was Lapierre, who scored the only goal of the game at 4:35 of the third period on a sensational play. Kevin Bieksa had the puck at the right point and saw Thomas come well out to challenge him as he prepared to shoot. There was a scrum of players in front, but off to the back side was Lapierre. Bieksa,

Defenceman Kevin Bieska watches as goalie Roberto Luongo makes a fine glove save.

86

Stanley Cup Final — Vancouver Canucks vs. Boston Bruins

Boston's Andrew Ference lets go a shot that Chris Higgins tries to block.

who must have played some snooker in his day, fired a shot off the end boards that came out the other side of the net, right onto Lapierre's stick. He fired quickly, and Thomas dove back to snare the puck—but it had already crossed the goal line.

It was Vancouver's first goal in nearly 111 minutes of Cup Final play and came after Thomas had stoned Lapierre on a sure goal off the rush before the Canucks established possession in the Boston end.

"He's coming out far so the only way to make him pay is to put pucks off the boards and hope they bounce into the slot," Bieksa explained. "I'm trying just to put it off the wall and hope it got a bounce. Obviously (I'm) not a geometry whiz, so I'm not sure exactly where but I was hoping it would bounce somewhere in front of the net. It bounced to our stick."

That was all the scoring Luongo needed. He played great down the stretch, including a huge left pad save

off a Johnny Boychuk point shot through traffic with a couple of minutes left in the game.

Again, though, as had been the case all playoffs, the Bruins power play was a culprit on this night. Boston was given the first three power plays of the game yet couldn't cash in at a time when an early goal would have had a huge impact of the game.

"We get criticized and scrutinized more than anybody I think, but that's what makes us professionals," Vancouver's Ryan Kesler added. "We deal with it. We're a tight-knit group in here, and we have each other's backs. We're a family, and I don't think there is a guy in here for one second saying that we didn't believe in Lu because we all believed in him."

And now, the Canucks had a chance to take their energy, and Luongo's goaltending, and try to win the Stanley Cup. But they had to do it in inhospitable Boston.

Stanley Cup Final — Vancouver Canucks vs. Boston Bruins

87

Too late. Boston goalie Tim Thomas reaches back to snare the puck, but it has already crossed the goal line for the only goal of the game.

88

Stanley Cup Final — Vancouver Canucks vs. Boston Bruins

GAME SIX — *June 13, 2011*

Vancouver 2 at **Boston 5**

(series tied 3-3)

Perhaps there has never been a stranger Stanley Cup Final series in NHL history. The Vancouver Canucks, who had played such a disciplined, team-oriented game in three meetings in Rogers Arena during their three victories, simply fell apart in each of their three visits to TD Garden in three lop-sided losses.

And Canucks goalie Roberto Luongo, virtually unbeatable at home, was nothing short of disastrous on the road. Again this night he was chased from the crease, surrendering three early goals in a 5–2 loss.

In all, the Bruins scored four times in 4:14 of the early part of the game and waltzed to an easy victory to force a decisive seventh game.

The outcome might have been different had Henrik Sedin converted a superb slapshot pass from Kevin Bieksa on the first shift. It came from the point, bounced off the end boards and out the other side, just like Maxim Lapierre's goal in game five. As it was, the puck hopped over Sedin's stick. Things got worse when Mason Raymond was rammed backwards into the boards by Johnny Boychuk and left the game from what looked a painful tail-bone injury.

Soon after, the Boston barrage began.

Jannik Hansen hits the side of the net on this breakaway as goalie Tim Thomas outwaits him on the deke.

Stanley Cup Final — Vancouver Canucks vs. Boston Bruins

89

David Krejci buries a cross-crease pass from Mark Recchi on a five-on-three in the third period.

Brad Marchand got some open ice down the right side, and as he barrelled in on goal he roofed a shot over the glove of Luongo at 5:35 to open the scoring. Luongo was on his knees long before the shot left Marchand's stick. Just thirty-five seconds later, Milan Lucic knifed a shot that squirted between Luongo's pads and rolled over the goal line. Coach Alain Vigneault might have given his goalie the hook then because it was clear Luongo wasn't on his game, but he waited one more goal.

That came just two minutes later when an Andrew Ference point shot beat the goalie cleanly. Cory Schneider came in and was sensational the rest of the way, although the Bruins did make it 4–0 soon after

when Michael Ryder tipped Tomas Kaberle's point shot off the post and in. Vigneault called a timeout, and although it had a calming effect, the damage had been done.

Vancouver might have gotten back in the game late in the first, but Jannik Hansen was only able to get off a weak shot on a breakaway. The Canucks continued to struggle on the power play in the series, failing to convert on two chances in the second and making it 0-for-20 in the series. They managed to get their first with the extra man just twenty-two seconds into the third, but that's as close as they got.

Henrik Sedin got that goal, moving into the slot, outwaiting Thomas, and roofing a backhand, but

90

Stanley Cup Final — Vancouver Canucks vs. Boston Bruins

Boston made in 5–1 during a five-on-three power play a few minutes later when David Krejci converted a great cross-crease pass from Mark Recchi.

Maxim Lapierre got a late goal for the Canucks to close out the scoring, and game seven was slated for two nights later. The Canucks had home ice, but the Bruins had the momentum. The outcome was undecided, but one thing was absolutely certain. The Cup would be in the building, and one team was going to skate off the ice with it.

"We've created ourselves another opportunity, and it's up to us to take advantage of it," said Boston coach Claude Julien. "But we've got to be hungrier than we have been the last three times in Vancouver."

The unflappable Luongo continued to exude confidence in the face of adversity. "I have to believe in myself, right? That's a big component of bouncing back and playing a good game," he suggested. "We're going to put what happened tonight behind us and get ready for what is going to be a dream as far as playing in game seven of the Stanley Cup Final."

Bruins players celebrate after their convincing 5-2 win to force a deciding game seven.

Stanley Cup Final — Vancouver Canucks vs. Boston Bruins

91

GAME SEVEN — *June 15, 2011*

Boston 4 at Vancouver 0
(***Boston*** wins series 4–3)

It wasn't meant to be. It was the last game of the year and the Stanley Cup was in the building. So, too, were Mason Raymond of Vancouver and Nathan Horton of Boston, two players badly injured but making the trip to the Rogers Arena for the grand finale. Boston hadn't won the Cup since 1972. Vancouver hadn't ever won the Cup since joining the league in 1970. A Canadian team hadn't won the Cup since Montreal in 1993, but Canada did win Olympic gold in this very building only sixteen months earlier—with Roberto Luongo in goal.

But the Bruins, losers of the first three games in Vancouver despite three dominating performances at home, came out and played a perfect home game on the road, dominating all over the ice and scoring the critical first goal to take the crowd out of the game.

Patrice Bergeron became just the twenty-fifth member of the Triple Gold Club, and he did so in style, scoring two goals in the first forty minutes to take the Boston Bruins to a 4–0 victory and the Stanley Cup. Brad Marchand also scored twice for the victors.

Most amazing, though, is that the Canucks, the highest scoring team in the regular season, scored just eight goals in seven games against the sensational Tim Thomas, named Conn Smythe Trophy winner after the game. The Bruins, meanwhile, counted twenty-three goals against an often shaky Roberto Luongo (who himself would have joined the TGC with a win).

The Boston Bruins were Stanley Cup champions for the first time in thirty-nine years. Interestingly, it was thirty-nine years between Cup wins in 1941 and 1970 as well.

Bergeron has now won the Stanley Cup, Olympic gold, and World Championship gold—the three requirements for Triple Gold Club membership.

Alexandre Burrows has a great scoring chance early with goalie Tim Thomas out of position, but Zdeno Chara in behind got his arm on the shot and saved a goal.

92

Stanley Cup Final — Vancouver Canucks vs. Boston Bruins

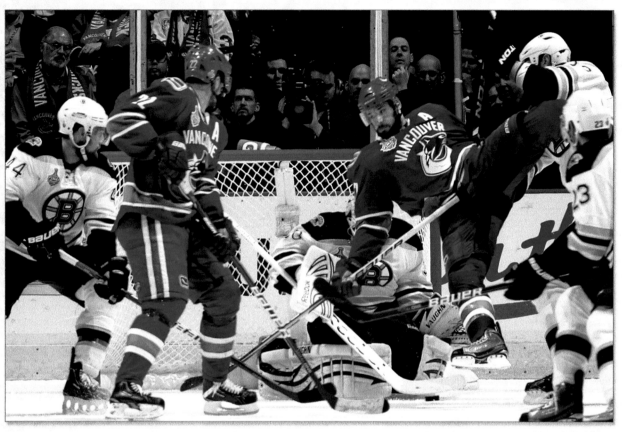

A scrum of players in front of Tim Thomas makes life difficult for the goalie, but he was perfect this night, stopping all 37 shots he faced.

The Canucks couldn't match the goaltending of Tim Thomas, couldn't score on the power play despite such huge success in the first three rounds of the playoffs, and couldn't match the Bruins' physical intensity.

The home team had scored the first goal of every game so far and won all six games of the series so far. Both teams, looking nervous, had a couple of good chances early that they couldn't convert. For the Bruins, David Krejci threw the puck into the crease where Luongo managed to swipe it away. For Vancouver, Henrik Sedin and Chris Higgins had the puck in front but couldn't get it past Tim Thomas.

As it turned out, for the first time in the series, the visiting team scored the game's first goal, and it was a dandy. Brad Marchand got the puck deep in the Vancouver end off a faceoff won by the Canucks, and after cycling in the corner he spotted Bergeron in the slot. Marchand made a superb backhand pass through three Vancouver players, and Bergeron snapped a one-timer off the far post and past a stunned Luongo at 14:37.

The goal silenced the crowd, but Ryan Kesler came back moments later with a great chance,however, Thomas again had perfect body position and made a tough save look easy. The period ended 1–0 for the Bruins, Boston scoring in the opening period of a road game for the first time in the four games of this series.

Boston played a sensational road period in the second, getting the puck deep and forechecking aggressively, making it tough for the Canucks even to get out of their own end. Vancouver had no luck on the slow ice as pucks bounced over their stick at the worst time, and the Bruins capitalized on their few scoring chances.

In the second, two more errors by Luongo sealed Vancouver's fate. He mishandled a routine point shot, and Marchand got the puck to one side of the net and wrapped it into the far side. Luongo had made the save, but his momentum carried the puck over the goal line.

Then, late in the period, Bergeron stole the puck at his blue-line with the Canucks on a power play. He tore down the ice, being chased by Sami Salo, who

Stanley Cup Final — Vancouver Canucks vs. Boston Bruins

93

was going to get a penalty, but Bergeron got a shot off, fell into the net, and took the puck with him as Luongo gave up on the play. That 3–0 goal at 17:35 was the fatal blow. Everyone knew Thomas was not about to surrender three goals in the final twenty minutes. Indeed, everyone knew he would be named Conn Smythe Trophy winner if the Bruins won the Cup (and perhaps even if they didn't).

The third period was all about shutting down the Canucks, which the Bruins did to perfection. Marchand got his second into an empty net as coach Alain Vigneault did what he could to get his team on the board. After the final horn, the Bruins poured onto the ice and celebrated a remarkable victory at the end of a rigourous and spectacular season.

The Canucks could only look back and wonder. The Sedins, so dominating all season, were completely neutralized by the Bruins. Ryan Kesler seemed to run out of gas, and Luongo was simply far weaker than his counterpart. Nevertheless, the Canucks made it to game seven of the Stanley Cup Final, and only two teams of thirty could boast as much.

Brad Marchand scores on a wraparound, surprising Roberto Luongo with the quick move.

94

Stanley Cup Final — Vancouver Canucks vs. Boston Bruins

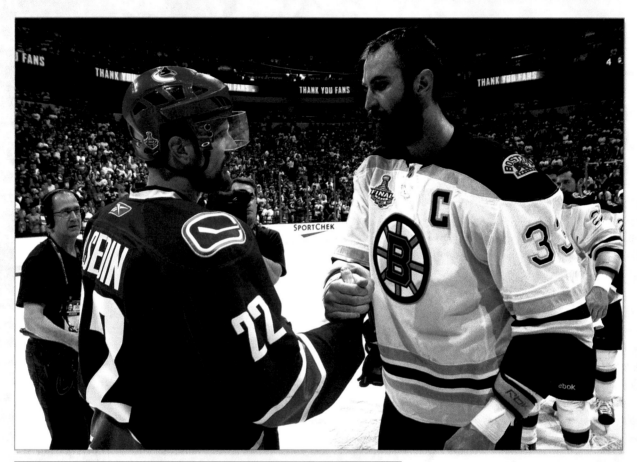

Daniel Sedin congratulates Boston captain Zdeno Chara after a tense and dramatic Stanley Cup Final; the two goalies, Roberto Luongo (left) and Tim Thomas, exchange handshakes after Boston's win.

Stanley Cup Final — Vancouver Canucks vs. Boston Bruins

95

There wasn't much indication at the start of the 1981–82 season that this Vancouver Canucks team was Stanley Cup ready. In fact, they were playing in a Smythe Division with an Edmonton Oilers' team that featured Gretzky et al. and any other team going all the way was a distant thought. During the regular season, the Oilers finished in first place in the division, winning forty-eight games, scoring an all-time record of 417 goals, and looking to be the dominant favourites to topple the New York Islanders who had won the Cup in 1980 and 1981.

But the Oilers were young and cocky and failed to take their first-round opponent seriously enough as the playoffs began, losing to the L.A. Kings, 7–4, in the fifth and deciding game of a series that included a 10–8 loss and blowing a 5–0 lead in another game. The Canucks, meanwhile, despite having a 30–33–17 record in the regular season, swept Calgary in three games of their preliminary-round series, thanks to the great play of Richard Brodeur, the goalie soon dubbed "King Richard."

Vancouver carried that momentum—and Brodeur's great goaltending—all the way to the final. In the next round, the Canucks took out the Kings, winning the last three games in a row of the five-game series and setting up a semi-final, best-of-seven with Chicago. The Canucks won the opener of that series, 2–1 in overtime at the Stadium, thanks to a goal by Jim Nill midway through the second extra period.

It was the next game that changed the history of the playoffs, and, indeed, the history of hockey in the NHL and around the world. The records show that the Hawks won the game, 4–1, to even the series, but what it doesn't show was the frustration Vancouver coach Roger Neilson felt towards the officiating. Emotions got the better of him late in the game after a series of Canucks' penalties. Chicago scored two late goals on the power play, and after the second, by Denis Savard, Neilson took a white towel from the bench, draped it on the butt end of a player's stick, and hoisted it high in the air, the captain of this hockey ship signaling surrender. Some of his players followed suit, resulting in a bench minor handed out by referee Bob Myers, and, of course, the image made all the headlines in the next day's newspapers.

Games three and four in the series were back in Vancouver, and thousands of fans brought their own white towels in support of their team. Thus began a tradition that sees many teams distribute towels of their team's colours to wave in unison whenever the mood strikes.

The Canucks, meanwhile, rode their emotions to another five-game series win over Chicago and faced the Islanders in the Stanley Cup Final. Unfortunately for Vancouver, the Islanders were the dominant team in the league and won in four straight games, but the Canucks gave their fans a taste of what the good life of the Stanley Cup was all about.

New York Islanders star Bryan Trottier is stopped by "King Richard" Brodeur during the 1982 Stanley Cup Final.

Much like in 1982, the 1994 Vancouver Canucks run to the Stanley Cup Final was more of a surprise than an expected result. After all, the team was barely above .500 in the standings, finishing the 84-game schedule with a record of 41–40–3. Although good for second in the Pacific Division, this was the weaker of the two divisions in the Western Conference and the Canucks ranked only seventh heading into the playoffs.

Just as Richard Brodeur had done in 1982, though, the Canucks got spectacular goaltending from Kirk McLean in 1994, proving again the value of the masked man in the playoffs. No more was his importance evident than the first series, against Calgary, the second-ranked team in the conference. Calgary won three of the first four games to take a commanding lead, looking certain to advance. The series, however, went seven games, and the last three went to overtime, Vancouver winning all of them.

Game seven was the most intense, of course, and McLean made the greatest save of his career in that overtime, against Robert Reichel who took a great pass from Theo Fleury only to see McLean stack the pads sliding to the back side of his goal and keep the game tied. Early in the second overtime, Pavel Bure scored on a breakaway, giving the Canucks the series win. It came off a sensational pass from Jeff Brown and finished with a great deke on goalie Mike Vernon.

As in 1982, the next two series were relatively easy for the Canucks as they won both in five games, first against Dallas and then Toronto. Both wins came during a new playoff format in which teams played two games in the city with home-ice advantage, then three games in the opponents' city, then two more, if necessary, back in the higher-ranked team's city. The result was that the visitor actually had an advantage because if it won just one of the first two games it could go home and clinch the series. The format was short-lived, but it served Vancouver well in 1994.

For the Stanley Cup Final, though, the format reverted to the standard 2–2–1–1–1, and this gave the New York Rangers the well-earned advantage. Teams split the first two games at Madison Square Garden, and then the Rangers pulled ahead, winning both games in Vancouver and almost certainly clinching the Cup. But the Canucks fought back, doubling New York, 6–3, with the Cup in the building at MSG, and then forcing a game seven with a 4–1 win at home in game six.

The magic run couldn't continue, though, and Mark Messier's Rangers won the finale, 3–2, to win the Cup, leaving Vancouver coach Pat Quinn a runner-up again (having taken Philadelphia to the Stanley Cup Final in 1980). The Canucks had made it twice to the Stanley Cup Final—and twice lost to a team from New York.

The Rangers and Canucks played seven games to determine the 1994 Cup champs, the New Yorkers coming out on top, 3-2 in the finale.

In the summer of 1914, an agreement was reached between the National Hockey Association (precursor to the NHL) and the Pacific Coast Hockey Association (PCHA) to hold a best-of-three series between the leagues' two champions to determine the winner of the Stanley Cup. Although the PCHA was only four years old, it had wooed many of the best players in the country away from the NHA and was a clear, if not equal, competitor.

The NHA had two teams in Toronto, two in Montreal, and one each in Ottawa and Quebec, while the PCHA had only three teams, the Vancouver Millionaires, Portland Rosebuds, and Victoria Aristocrats. In 1914–15, Vancouver faced the Ottawa Senators for the Cup, all games being played at the Denman Arena in Vancouver.

The Millionaires were famous for their sweaters, which featured a large and thick "V" inside which was written the city name. Coached by Frank Patrick, they overwhelmed Ottawa, winning 6–2, 8–3, and 12–3. Barney Stanley was the hero in the final game, scoring six goals.

The PCHA put up a good fight in the coming years. The Rosebuds lost to the Montreal Canadiens the next year, losing on a late goal in game five. In 1916–17, the Seattle Metropolitans, who had joined in 1915, became the first U.S. team to win, and the year after the Millionaires lost to the Toronto Arenas in five games, the first year of the NHL's existence.

The Millionaires also went to the Stanley Cup Final in 1921 and 1922, after which they changed their name to Maroons. The Maroons lost a series to Ottawa in 1923 for the Cup, and lost again in 1924 and 1926. This was the last time a non-NHL team competed for the Cup, the NHL becoming by far and away the top league in the country by this time. But that win by the Millionaires in 1915 remains the only time the city won the Stanley Cup.

	GP	W	L	T/OT	GF	GA	Pts
1970-71	78	24	46	8	229	296	56
1971-72	78	20	50	8	203	297	48
1972-73	78	22	47	9	233	339	53
1973-74	78	24	43	11	224	296	59
1974-75	80	38	32	10	271	254	86
1975-76	80	33	32	15	271	272	81
1976-77	80	25	42	13	235	294	63
1977-78	80	20	43	17	239	320	57
1978-79	80	25	42	13	217	291	63
1979-80	80	27	37	16	256	281	70
1980-81	80	28	32	20	289	301	76
1981-82	80	30	33	17	290	286	77
1982-83	80	30	35	15	303	309	75
1983-84	80	32	39	9	306	328	73
1984-85	80	25	46	9	284	401	59
1985-86	80	23	44	13	282	333	59
1986-87	80	29	43	8	282	314	66
1987-88	80	25	46	9	272	320	59
1988-89	80	33	39	8	251	253	74
1989-90	80	25	41	14	245	306	64
1990-91	80	28	43	9	243	315	65
1991-92	80	42	26	12	285	250	96
1992-93	84	46	29	9	346	278	101
1993-94	84	41	40	3	279	276	85
1994-95	48	18	18	12	153	148	48
1995-96	82	32	35	15	278	278	79
1996-97	82	35	40	7	257	273	77
1997-98	82	25	43	14	224	273	64
1998-99	82	23	47	12	192	258	58
1999-2000	82	30	29	15	227	237	83
2000-01	82	36	29	11	239	238	90
2001-02	82	42	30	7	254	211	94
2002-03	82	45	23	13	264	208	104
2003-04	82	43	24	10	235	194	101
2004-05			NO SEASON				
2005-06	82	42	32	8	256	255	92
2006-07	82	49	26	7	222	201	105
2007-08	82	39	33	10	213	215	88
2008-09	82	45	27	10	246	220	100
2009-10	82	49	28	5	272	222	103
2010-11	82	54	19	9	262	185	117

PREVIOUS PLAYOFF RESULTS

1970-71	DNQ
1971-72	DNQ
1972-73	DNQ
1973-74	DNQ

1974-75

April 13   Vancouver 2 at Montreal 6
April 15   Vancouver 2 at Montreal 1
April 17   Montreal 4 at Vancouver 1
April 19   Montreal 4 at Vancouver 0
April 22   Vancouver 4 at Montreal 5 (17:06 OT)
Montreal wins best-of-seven 4-1

1975-76

April 6   Vancouver 3 at NY Islanders 5
April 8   NY Islanders 3 at Vancouver 1
NY Islanders win best-of-three 2-0

1976-77	DNQ
1977-78	DNQ

1978-79

April 10   Vancouver 3 at Philadelphia 2
April 12   Philadelphia 6 at Vancouver 4
April 14   Vancouver 2 at Philadelphia 7
Philadelphia wins best-of-three 2-1

1979-80

April 8   Vancouver 1 at Buffalo 2
April 9   Vancouver 0 at Buffalo 6
April 11   Buffalo 4 at Vancouver 5
April 12   Buffalo 3 at Vancouver 1
Buffalo wins best-of-five 3-1

1980-81

April 8   Vancouver 2 at Buffalo 3 (5:00 OT)
April 9   Vancouver 2 at Buffalo 5
April 11   Buffalo 5 at Vancouver 3
Buffalo wins best-of-five 3-0

1981-82

April 7   Calgary 3 at Vancouver 5
April 8   Calgary 1 at Vancouver 2 (14:20 OT)
April 10   Vancouver 3 at Calgary 1
Vancouver wins best-of-five 3-0

April 15   Los Angeles 2 at Vancouver 3
April 16   Los Angeles 3 at Vancouver 2
           (4:33 OT)
April 18   Vancouver 4 at Los Angeles 3
April 19   Vancouver 5 at Los Angeles 4

April 21   Los Angeles 2 at Vancouver 5
Vancouver wins best-of-seven 4-1

April 27   Vancouver 2 at Chicago 1 (28:28 OT)
April 29   Vancouver 1 at Chicago 4
May 1   Chicago 3 at Vancouver 4
May 4   Chicago 3 at Vancouver 5
May 6   Vancouver 6 at Chicago 2
Vancouver wins best-of-seven 4-1

May 8   Vancouver 5 at NY Islanders 6
           (19:58 OT)
May 11   Vancouver 4 at NY Islanders 6
Mat 13   NY Islanders 3 at Vancouver 0
May 16   NY Islanders 3 at Vancouver 1
NY Islanders win best-of-seven 4-0

1982-83

April 6   Vancouver 3 at Calgary 4 (12:27 OT)
April 7   Vancouver 3 at Calgary 5
April 9   Calgary 4 at Vancouver 5
April 10   Calgary 4 at Vancouver 3 (1:06 OT)
Calgary wins best-of-five 3-1

1983-84

April 4   Vancouver 3 at Calgary 5
April 5   Vancouver 2 at Calgary 4
April 7   Calgary 0 at Vancouver 7
April 8   Calgary 5 at Vancouver 1
Calgary wins best-of-five 3-1

1984-85   DNQ

1985-86

April 9   Vancouver 3 at Edmonton 7
April 10   Vancouver 1 at Edmonton 5
April 12   Edmonton 5 at Vancouver 1
Edmonton wins best-of-seven 3-0

1986-87   DNQ

1987-88   DNQ

1988-89

April 5   Vancouver 4 at Calgary 3 (2:47 OT)
April 6   Vancouver 2 at Calgary 5
April 8   Calgary 4 at Vancouver 0
April 9   Calgary 3 at Vancouver 5
April 11   Vancouver 0 at Calgary 4
April 13   Calgary 3 at Vancouver 6
April 15   Vancouver 3 at Calgary 4 (19:21 OT)
Calgary wins best-of-seven 4-3

1989-90   DNQ

1990-91

April 4   Vancouver 6 at Los Angeles 5
April 6   Vancouver 2 at Los Angeles 3
           (11:08 OT)
April 8   Los Angeles 1 at Vancouver 2
           (3:12 OT)
April 10   Los Angeles 6 at Vancouver 1
April 12   Vancouver 4 at Los Angeles 7
April 14   Los Angeles 4 at Vancouver 1
Los Angeles wins best-of-seven 4-2

1991-92

April 18   Winnipeg 3 at Vancouver 2
April 20   Winnipeg 2 at Vancouver 3
April 22   Vancouver 2 at Winnipeg 4
April 24   Vancouver 1 at Winnipeg 3
April 26   Winnipeg 2 at Vancouver 8
April 28   Vancouver 8 at Winnipeg 3
April 30   Winnipeg 0 at Vancouver 5
Vancouver wins best-of-seven 4-3

May 3   Edmonton 4 at Vancouver 3 (8:36 OT)
May 4   Edmonton 0 at Vancouver 4
May 6   Vancouver 2 at Edmonton 5
May 8   Vancouver 2 at Edmonton 3
May 10   Edmonton 3 at Vancouver 4
May 12   Vancouver 0 at Edmonton 3
Edmonton wins best-of-seven 4-2

1992-93

April 19   Winnipeg 2 at Vancouver 4
April 21   Winnipeg 2 at Vancouver 3
April 23   Vancouver 4 at Winnipeg 5
April 25   Vancouver 3 at Winnipeg 1
April 27   Winnipeg 4 at Vancouver 3 (6:18 OT)
April 29   Vancouver 4 at Winnipeg 3 (4:30 OT)
Vancouver wins best-of-seven 4-2

May 2   Los Angeles 2 at Vancouver 5
May 5   Los Angeles 6 at Vancouver 3
May 7   Vancouver 4 at Los Angeles 7
May 9   Vancouver 7 at Los Angeles 2
May 11   Los Angeles 4 at Vancouver 3
           (26:31 OT)
May 13   Vancouver 3 at Los Angeles 5
Los Angeles wins best-of-seven 4-2

1993-94

April 18   Vancouver 5 at Calgary 0
April 20   Vancouver 5 at Calgary 7
April 22   Calgary 4 at Vancouver 2

April 24   Calgary 3 at Vancouver 2
April 26   Vancouver 2 at Calgary 1 (7:15 OT)
April 28   Calgary 2 at Vancouver 3 (16:43 OT)
April 30   Vancouver 4 at Calgary 3 (22:20 OT)
Vancouver wins best-of-seven 4-3

May 2   Vancouver 6 at Dallas 4
May 4   Vancouver 3 at Dallas 0
May 6   Dallas 4 at Vancouver 3
May 8   Dallas 1 at Vancouver 2 (11:01 OT)
May 10   Dallas 2 at Vancouver 4
Vancouver wins best-of-seven 4-1

May 16   Vancouver 2 at Toronto 3 (16:55 OT)
May 18   Vancouver 4 at Toronto 3
May 20   Toronto 0 at Vancouver 4
May 22   Toronto 0 at Vancouver 2
May 24   Toronto 3 at Vancouver 4 (20:14 OT)
Vancouver wins best-of-seven 4-1

May 31   Vancouver 3 at NY Rangers 2
           (19:26 OT)
June 2   Vancouver 1 at NY Rangers 3
June 4   NY Rangers 5 at Vancouver 1
June 7   NY Rangers 4 at Vancouver 2
June 9   Vancouver 6 at NY Rangers 3
June 11   NY Rangers 1 at Vancouver 4
June 14   Vancouver 2 at NY Rangers 3
NY Rangers wins best-of-seven 4-3

1994-95

May 7   Vancouver 1 at St. Louis 2
May 9   Vancouver 5 at St. Louis 3
May 11   St. Louis 1 at Vancouver 6
May 13   St. Louis 5 at Vancouver 2
May 15   Vancouver 6 at St. Louis 5 (1:48 OT)
May 17   St. Louis 8 at Vancouver 2
May 19   Vancouver 5 at St. Louis 3
Vancouver wins best-of-seven 4-3

May 21   Vancouver 1 at Chicago 2 (9:04 OT)
May 23   Vancouver 0 at Chicago 2
May 25   Chicago 3 at Vancouver 2 (6:22 OT)
May 27   Chicago 4 at Vancouver 3 (5:35 OT)
Chicago wins best-of-seven 4-0

1995-96
April 16   Vancouver 2 at Colorado 5
April 18   Vancouver 5 at Colorado 4
April 20   Colorado 4 at Vancouver 0
April 22   Colorado 3 at Vancouver 4
April 25   Vancouver 4 at Colorado 5 (0:51)
April 27   Colorado 3 at Vancouver 2
Colorado wins best-of-seven 4-2

1996-97	DNQ
1997-98	DNQ
1998-99	DNQ
1999-2000	DNQ

2000-01

April 12   Vancouver 4 at Colorado 5
April 14   Vancouver 1 at Colorado 2
April 16   Colorado 4 at Vancouver 3 (2:50 OT)
April 18   Colorado 5 at Vancouver 1
Colorado wins best-of-seven 4-0

2001-02

April 17   Vancouver 4 at Detroit 3 (13:59 OT)
April 19   Vancouver 5 at Detroit 2
April 21   Detroit 3 at Vancouver 1
April 23   Detroit 4 at Vancouver 2
April 25   Vancouver 0 at Detroit 4
April 27   Detroit 6 at Vancouver 4
Detroit wins best-of-seven 4-2

2002-03

April 10   St. Louis 6 at Vancouver 0
April 12   St. Louis 1 at Vancouver 2
April 14   Vancouver 1 at St. Louis 3
April 16   Vancouver 1 at St. Louis 4
April 18   St. Louis 3 at Vancouver 5
April 20   Vancouver 4 at St. Louis 3
April 22   St. Louis 1 at Vancouver 4
Vancouver wins best-of-seven 4-3

April 25   Minnesota 3 at Vancouver 4 (3:42 OT)
April 27   Minnesota 3 at Vancouver 2
April 29   Vancouver 3 at Minnesota 2
May 2   Vancouver 3 at Minnesota 2 (15:52 OT)
May 5   Minnesota 7 at Vancouver 2
May 7   Vancouver 1 at Minnesota 5
May 8   Minnesota 4 at Vancouver 2
Minnesota wins best-of-seven 4-3

2003-04

April 7   Calgary 3 at Vancouver 5
April 9   Calgary 2 at Vancouver 1
April 11   Vancouver 2 at Calgary 1
April 13   Vancouver 0 at Calgary 4
April 15   Calgary 2 at Vancouver 1
April 17   Vancouver 5 at Calgary 4 (42:28 OT)
April 19   Calgary 3 at Vancouver 2 (1:25 OT)
Calgary wins best-of-seven 4-3

2004-05	NO SEASON
2005-06	DNQ

2006-07

April 11   Dallas 4 at Vancouver 5
April 13   Dallas 2 at Vancouver 0
April 15   Vancouver 2 at Dallas 1 (7:47 OT)
April 17   Vancouver 2 at Dallas 1
April 19   Dallas 1 at Vancouver 0 (6:22 OT)
April 21   Vancouver 0 at Dallas 2
April 23   Dallas 1 at Vancouver 4
Vancouver wins best-of-seven 4-3

April 25   Vancouver 1 at Anaheim 5
April 27   Vancouver 2 at Anaheim 1 (27:49 OT)
April 29   Anaheim 3 at Vancouver 2
May 1   Anaheim 3 at Vancouver 2 (2:07 OT)
May 3   Vancouver 1 at Anaheim 2 (24:30 OT)
Anaheim wins best-of-seven 4-1

2007-08	DNQ

2008-09

April 15   St. Louis 1 at Vancouver 2
April 17   St. Louis 0 at Vancouver 3
April 19   Vancouver 3 at St. Louis 2
April 21   Vancouver 3 at St. Louis 2 (19:41 OT)
Vancouver wins best-of-seven 4-0

April 30   Chicago 3 at Vancouver 5
May 2   Chicago 6 at Vancouver 3
May 5   Vancouver 3 at Chicago 1
May 7   Vancouver 1 at Chicago 2 (2:52 OT)
May 9   Chicago 4 at Vancouver 2
May 11   Vancouver 5 at Chicago 7
Chicago wins best-of-seven 4-2

2009-10

April 15   Los Angeles 2 at Vancouver 3 (8:52 OT)
April 17   Los Angeles 3 at Vancouver 2 (7:28 OT)
April 19   Vancouver 3 at Los Angeles 5
April 21   Vancouver 6 at Los Angeles 4
April 23   Los Angeles 2 at Vancouver 7
April 25   Vancouver 4 at Los Angeles 2
Vancouver wins best-of-seven 4-2

May 1   Vancouver 5 at Chicago 1
May 3   Vancouver 2 at Chicago 4
May 5   Chicago 5 at Vancouver 2
May 7   Chicago 7 at Vancouver 4
May 9   Vancouver 4 at Chicago 1
May 11   Chicago 5 at Vancouver 1
Chicago wins best-of-seven 4-2

CANUCKS IN THE ALL-STAR GAME (CHRONOLOGICAL)

Player	Year Team	G	A	P	Pim
Goalie	*Year Team*	*Mins*	*GA*		*W/L*
Dale Tallon	1971 East	0	0	0	0
Dale Tallon	1972 East	0	0	0	0
Bobby Schmautz	1973 East	1	0	1	0
Jocelyn Guevremont	1974 East	0	0	0	0
Bobby Schmautz	1974 East	0	0	0	0
Tracy Pratt	1975 Campbell	0	0	0	0
Gary Smith	*1975 Campbell*	*30:43*	*4*		*nd*
Dennis Ververgaert	1976 Campbell	2	0	2	0
Harold Snepsts	1977 Campbell	0	0	0	0
Dennis Ververgaert	1978 Campbell	0	0	0	0
Lars Lindgren	1980 Campbell	0	0	0	0
Tiger Williams	1981 Campbell	0	0	0	0
Kevin McCarthy	1981 Campbell	0	0	0	0
Harold Snepsts	1982 Campbell	0	0	0	0
John Garrett	*1983 Campbell*	*29:56*	*1*		*W*
Darcy Rota	1984 Campbell	1	1	2	0
Thomas Gradin	1985 Campbell	0	0	0	0
Tony Tanti	1986 Campbell	1	0	1	0
Greg Adams	1988 Campbell	0	0	0	0
Paul Reinhart	1989 Campbell	0	0	0	0
Kirk McLean	*1990 Campbell*	*30:46*	*4*		*nd*
Trevor Linden	1991 Campbell	0	0	0	0
Kirk McLean	*1992 Campbell*	*20:00*	*3*		*nd*
Trevor Linden	1992 Campbell	1	1	2	0
Pavel Bure	1993 Campbell	2	0	2	0
Pavel Bure	1994 Western	0	2	2	0
Alexander Mogilny	1996 Western	0	1	1	0
Pavel Bure	1997 Western	2	1	3	0
Pavel Bure	1998 World	0	1	1	0
Mark Messier	1998 North America	1	1	2	0

Player	Year Team	G	A	P	Pim
Goalie	*Year Team*	*Mins*	*GA*		*W/L*
Mattias Ohlund	1999 World	1	1	2	0
Markus Naslund	1999 World	0	1	1	0
Mark Messier	2000 North America	0	1	1	0
Ed Jovanovski	2001 North America	0	1	1	0
Markus Naslund	2001 World	1	1	2	0
Ed Jovanovski	2002 North America	1	0	1	0
Markus Naslund	2002 World	2	1	3	0
Ed Jovanovski	2003 Western	1	0	1	0
Todd Bertuzzi	2003 Western	0	0	0	0
Markus Naslund	2003 Western	0	1	1	0
Todd Bertuzzi	2004 Western	0	2	2	0
Markus Naslund	2004 Western	0	3	3	0
Roberto Luongo	*2007 Western*	*20:00*	*3*		*nd*
Henrik Sedin	2008 Western	0	2	2	0
Roberto Luongo	*2009 Western*	*25:00*	*3*		*L*
Ryan Kesler	2011 Team Staal	0	0	0	0
Henrik Sedin	2011 Team Lidstrom	0	2	2	0
Daniel Sedin	2011 Team Staal	0	1	1	0

All-Star Teams

1991-92	Second	Goal	Kirk McLean
1993-94	First	Right Wing	Pavel Bure
1995-96	Second	Right Wing	Alexander Mogilny
2002-03	First	Right Wing	Todd Bertuzzi
2003-04	First	Left Wing	Markus Naslund
2006-07	Second	Goal	Roberto Luongo
2009-10	First	Centre	Henrik Sedin
2009-10	Second	Left Wing	Daniel Sedin

VANCOUVER CANUCKS IN THE HOCKEY HALL OF FAME

Roger Neilson (2002)

Cam Neely (2005)

Mark Messier (2007)

Igor Larionov (2008)

NUMBERS RETIRED BY THE VANCOUVER CANUCKS

11   Wayne Maki*

12   Stan Smyl

16   Trevor Linden

19   Markus Naslund

*Wayne Maki's number was unofficially retired by the Canucks after his death in 1974.

VANCOUVER CANUCKS TROPHY WINNERS

Art Ross Trophy

2009-10   Henrik Sedin
2010-11   Daniel Sedin

Hart Trophy

2009-10   Henrik Sedin

Calder Trophy

1991-92   Pavel Bure

King Clancy Trophy

1996-97   Trevor Linden

Lester B. Pearson Award

2002-03   Markus Naslund

Jack Adams Award

1991-92   Pat Quinn
2006-07   Alain Vigneault

William M. Jennings Trophy

2010-11   Roberto Luongo and
Cory Schneider

1970

2	Dale Tallon
16	Jim Hargreaves
30	Ed Dyck
44	Brent Taylor
58	Bill McFadden
72	Dave Gilmour

1971

3	Jocelyn Guevrement
17	Bobby Lalonde
39	Richard Lemieux
59	Mike McNiven
73	Tom Steeves
87	Bill Green
101	Norm Cherry
102	Bob Murphy

1972

3	Don Lever
19	Brian McSheffrey
35	Paul Raymer
51	Ron Homenuke
67	Larry Bolonchuk
83	Dave McClelland
99	Danny Gloor
115	Dennis McCord
131	Steve Stone

1973

3	Dennis Ververgaert
9	Bob Dailey
19	Paulin Bordeleau
35	Paul Sheard
51	Keith Mackie
67	Paul O'Neil
83	Jim Cowell
99	Clay Hebenton
115	John Senkpiel
131	Peter Folco
147	Terry McDougall

1974

23	Ron Sedlbauer
41	John Hughes
59	Harold Snepsts
77	Mike Rogers
95	Andy Spruce
113	Jim Clarke
130	Robbie Watt
147	Marc Gaudreault

1975

10	Rick Blight
28	Brad Gassoff
46	Norm LaPointe
64	Glen Richardson
82	Doug Murray
100	Bob Watson

118	Brian Shmyr
136	Allan Fleck
152	Bob McNeice
182	Sid Veysey

1976

26	Bob Manno
44	Rob Flockhart
62	Elmer Ray
80	Dick Durston
98	Rob Tudor
114	Brad Rhiness
122	Stu Ostlund

1977

4	Jere Gillis
22	Jeff Bandura
40	Glen Hanlon
56	Dave Morrow
58	Murray Bannerman
76	Steve Hazlett
94	Brian Drumm
112	Ray Creasey

1978

4	Bill Derlago
22	Curt Fraser
40	Stan Smyl
56	Harold Luckner
57	Brad Smith
90	Gerry Minor
107	Dave Ross
124	Steve O'Neill
141	Charlie Antetomaso
158	Rick Martens

1979

5	Rick Vaive
26	Brent Ashton
47	Ken Ellacott
68	Arthur Rutland
89	Dirk Graham
110	Shane Swan

1980

7	Rick Lanz
49	Andy Schliebener
70	Marc Crawford
91	Darrell May
112	Ken Berry
133	Doug Lidster
154	John O'Connor
175	Patrik Sundstrom
196	Grant Martin

1981

10	Garth Butcher
52	Jean-Marc Lanthier
73	Wendell Young

105	Moe Lemay
115	Stu Kulak
136	Bruce Holloway
157	Petri Skriko
178	Frank Caprice
199	Rejean Vignola

1982

11	Michel Petit
53	Yves Lapointe
71	Shawn Kilroy
116	Taylor Hall
137	Parie Proft
158	Newell Brown
179	Don McLaren
200	Al Raymond
221	Steve Driscoll
242	Shawn Green

1983

9	Cam Neely
30	David Bruce
50	Scott Tottle
70	Tim Lorenz
90	Doug Quinn
110	Dave Lowry
130	Terry Maki
150	John Labatt
170	Allan Measures
190	Roger Grillo
210	Steve Kayser
230	Jay Mazur

1984

10	J.J. Daigneault
31	Jeff Rohlicek
52	Dave Saunders
55	Landis Chaulk
58	Mike Stevens
73	Brian Bertuzzi
94	Brett MacDonald
115	Jeff Korchinski
136	Blaine Chrest
157	Jim Agnew
178	Rex Grant
198	Ed Lowney
219	Doug Clarke
239	Ed Kister

1985

4	Jim Sandlak
25	Troy Gamble
46	Shane Doyle
67	Randy Siska
88	Robert Kron
109	Martin Hrstka
130	Brian McFarlane
151	Hakan Ahlund
172	Curtis Hunt

193	Carl Valimont
214	Igor Larionov
235	Darren Taylor

1986

7	Dan Woodley
49	Don Gibson
70	Ronnie Stern
91	Eric Murano
112	Steve Herniman
133	Jon Helgeson
154	Jeff Noble
175	Matt Merten
196	Marc Lyons
217	Todd Hawkins
238	Vladimir Krutov

1987

24	Rob Murphy
45	Steve Veilleux
66	Doug Torrel
87	Sean Fabian
108	Garry Valk
129	Todd Fanning
150	Viktor Tumeneu
171	Craig Daly
192	John Fletcher
213	Roger Hansson
233	Neil Eisenhut
234	Matt Evo

1988

2	Trevor Linden
33	Leif Rohlin
44	Dane Jackson
107	Corrie D'Alessio
122	Phil von Stefenelli
128	Dixon Ward
149	Greg Geldart
170	Roger Akerstrom
191	Paul Constantin
212	Chris Wolanin
233	Stefan Nilsson

1989

8	Jason Herter
29	Rob Woodward
71	Brett Hauer
113	Pavel Bure
134	Jim Revenberg
155	Rob Sangster
176	Sandy Moger
197	Gus Morschauser
218	Hayden O'Rear
239	Darcy Cahill
248	Jan Bergman

1990

2	Petr Nedved
18	Shawn Antoski
23	Jiri Slegr
65	Darin Bader
86	Gino Odjick
128	Daryl Filipek
149	Paul O'Hagan
170	Mike Cipriano
191	Troy Neumier
212	Tyler Ertel
233	Karri Kivi

1991

7	Alek Stojanov
29	Jassen Cullimore
51	Sean Pronger
95	Dan Kesa
117	Evgeni Namestnikov
139	Brent Thurston
161	Eric Johnson
183	David Neilson
205	Brad Barton
227	Jason Fitzsimmons
249	Xavier Majic

1992

21	Libor Polasek
40	Michael Peca
45	Mike Fountain
69	Jeff Connolly
93	Brent Tully
110	Brian Loney
117	Adrian Aucoin
141	Jason Clark
165	Scott Hollis
213	Sonny Mignacca
237	Mark Wotton
261	Aaron Boh

1993

20	Mike Wilson
46	Rick Girard
98	Dieter Kochan
124	Scott Walker
150	Troy Creurer
176	Evgeni Babariko
202	Sean Tallaire
254	Bert Robertsson
280	Sergei Tkachenko

1994

13	Mattias Ohlund
39	Robb Gordon
42	Dave Scatchard
65	Chad Allan
92	Mike Dubinsky
117	Yanick Dube

169	Yuri Kuznetsov
195	Rob Trumbley
221	Bill Muckalt
247	Tyson Nash
273	Robert Longpre

1995

40	Chris McAllister
61	Larry Courville
66	Peter Schaefer
92	Lloyd Shaw
120	Todd Norman
144	Brent Sopel
170	Stewart Bodtker
196	Tyler Willis
222	Jason Cugnet

1996

12	Josh Holden
75	Zenith Komarniski
93	Jonas Soling
121	Tyler Prosofsky
147	Nolan McDonald
175	Clint Cabana
201	Jeff Scissons
227	Lubomir Vaic

1997

10	Brad Ference
34	Ryan Bonni
36	Harold Druken
64	Kyle Freadrich
90	Chris Stanley
114	David Darguzas
117	Matt Cockell
144	Matt Cooke
148	Larry Shapley
171	Rod Leroux
201	Denis Martynyuk
227	Peter Brady

1998

4	Bryan Allen
31	Artem Chubarov
68	Jarkko Ruutu
81	Justin Morrison
90	Regan Darby
136	David Jonsson
140	Rick Bertran
149	Paul Cabana
177	Vincent Malts
204	Graig Mischler
219	Curtis Valentine
232	Jason Metcalfe

1999

2	Daniel Sedin
3	Henrik Sedin

69	Rene Vydareny
129	Ryan Thorpe
172	Josh Reed
189	Kevin Swanson
218	Markus Kankaanpera
271	Darrell Hay

2000

23	Nathan Smith
71	Thatcher Bell
93	Tim Branham
144	Pavel Duma
208	Brandon Reid
241	Nathan Barrett
272	Tim Smith

2001

16	R.J. Umberger
66	Fedor Fedorov
114	Evgeny Gladskikh
151	Kevin Bieksa
212	Jason King
245	Konstantin Mihailov

2002

49	Kiril Koltsov
55	Denis Grot
68	Brett Skinner
83	Lukas Mensator
114	John Laliberte
151	Rob McVicar
214	Marc-Andre Roy
223	Ilya Krikunov
247	Matt Violin
277	Thomas Nussli
278	Matt Gens

2003

23	Ryan Kesler
60	Marc-Andre Bernier
111	Brandon Nolan
128	Ty Morris
160	Nicklas Danielsson
190	Chad Brownlee
222	Francois-Pierre Guenette
252	Sergei Topol
254	Nathan McIver
285	Matthew Hansen

2004

26	Cory Schneider
91	Alexander Edler
111	Andrew Sarauer
159	Mike Brown
189	Julien Ellis-Plante
254	David Schulz
287	Jannik Hansen

2005

10	Luc Bourdon
51	Mason Raymond
114	Alexandre Vincent
138	Matt Butcher
185	Kris Fredheim
205	Mario Bliznak

2006

14	Michael Grabner
82	Daniel Rahimi
163	Sergei Shirokov
167	Juraj Simek
197	Evan Fuller

2007

25	Patrick White
33	Taylor Ellington
145	Charles-Antoine Messier
146	Ilya Kablukov
176	Taylor Matson
206	Dan Gendur

2008

10	Cody Hodgson
41	Yann Sauve
131	Prab Rai
161	Mats Froshaug
191	Morgan Clark

2009

22	Jordan Schroeder
53	Anton Rodin
83	Kevin Connauton
113	Jeremy Price
143	Peter Andersson
173	Joe Cannata
187	Steven Anthony

2010

115	Patrick McNally
145	Adam Polasek
172	Alex Friesen
175	Jonathan Iilahti
205	Sawyer Hannay

Alberts, Andrew

b. Minneapolis, Minnesota, June 30, 1981

Defence—shoots left

6'5"—218 lbs.

Drafted 179th overall by Boston in 2001

Big and strong and not particularly mobile, Alberts has made his reputation for play in his own end as a stay-at-home defenceman. He started his career playing in the USHL for two years, where he played well enough to be drafted by Boston in the summer of 2001. Before trying the NHL, though, he attended Boston College, and it was in NCAA hockey that he blossomed. He stayed four years, grew in size and strength, and by the time he graduated in 2005, he was a mature twenty-four-year-old.

Although the Bruins didn't make the playoffs during his first two seasons, he was impressive enough that USA Hockey invited him to play at the World Championship both years, and he gladly accepted. He learned how to adapt his game to the bigger ice and play the international game, gaining valuable experience. His career slowed in 2007–08, as he struggled to recover from a concussion, and he was traded to the Flyers prior to the next season. A year later, he signed as a free agent with the Hurricanes, but they traded him to Vancouver midway through the 2009–10 season.

Alberts had trouble adjusting at first, but near the start of the 2010–11 season, he re-dedicated himself to the game and took his play to a new level. He has been a key member of the blue-line corps ever since, blocking shots, standing up for teammates, and playing "smart hockey," as they say, in his own end.

Career Statistics	Regular Season					Playoffs				
	GP	G	A	P	Pim	GP	G	A	P	Pim
2005-06 BOS	73	1	6	7	68	DNQ				
2006-07 BOS	76	0	10	10	124	DNQ				
2007-08 BOS	35	0	2	2	39	2	0	0	0	0
2008-09 PHI	79	1	12	13	61	6	0	1	1	10
2009-10 CAR	62	2	8	10	74	--	--	--	--	--
2009-10 VAN	14	1	1	2	13	10	0	1	1	27
2010-11 VAN	42	1	6	7	41	for 2011 playoff stats see p. 19				
NHL Totals	381	6	45	51	420					

for 2011 playoff stats see p. 19

Ballard, Keith

b. Baudette, Minnesota, November 26, 1982

Defence—shoots left

5'11" 208 lbs.

Drafted 11th overall by Buffalo in 2002

One of the many graduates of the U.S. National Team Development Program, Ballard has played in many places during his career. After his year at the NTDP, he played in the USHL and then started his NCAA career with the University of Minnesota. At the end of his third year, 2003–04, he played for the U.S. at the World Championship in Prague, helping the team to win a bronze medal.

Ballard gave up his final year of college eligibility to start a career in the NHL, but it wasn't until his third team that he did so. After being drafted by Buffalo, the Sabres traded him to Colorado, and then from the Avalanche to Phoenix, before he had even played a game. To further complicate matters, the 2004–05 season was lost because of a lockout, so Ballard started his pro career in the AHL, with the Utah Grizzlies. Nonetheless, he made his NHL debut, with the Coyotes, in 2005–06, and for three years was a versatile and dependable defenceman for the team. He was a fine skater, but also a physical player inside his own blue-line, and he regularly logged more than twenty minutes of ice time a game.

The Coyotes missed the playoffs each season he was there, though, and they traded him to Florida with Nick Boynton and a draft choice for Olli Jokinen. The Panthers also missed the playoffs his two years there, but the upside for Ballard was that he was a frequent participant at the World Championship. In all, he

played in 2004, 2007, 2008, and 2009, gaining valuable experience despite the absence of the playoffs from his portfolio. He had previously played at the U18 and U20 tournaments as a teen.

Traded to the Canucks at draft time last year, Ballard had a frustrating 2010–11 regular season, suffering several injuries that kept him out of the lineup or forced him to play at a level below his best, but by the playoffs he was in excellent form.

Career Statistics	Regular Season					Playoffs				
	GP	G	A	P	Pim	GP	G	A	P	Pim
2005-06 PHO	82	8	31	39	99			DNQ		
2006-07 PHO	69	5	22	27	59			DNQ		
2007-08 PHO	82	6	15	21	85			DNQ		
2008-09 FLA	82	6	28	34	72			DNQ		
2009-10 FLA	82	8	20	28	88			DNQ		
2010-11 VAN	75	2	5	7	53		for 2011 playoff stats see p. 19			
NHL Totals	462	35	121	156	456					

Bieksa, Kevin

b. Grimsby, Ontario, June 16, 1981

Defence—shoots right

6'1" 198 lbs.

Drafted 151st overall by Vancouver in 2001

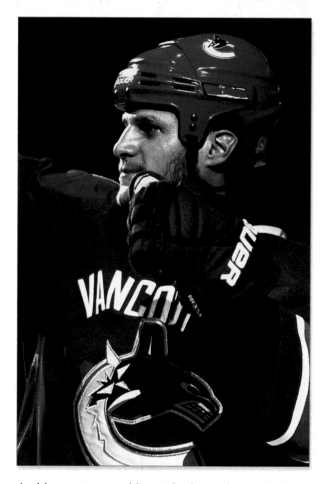

An outstanding junior prospect some fifteen years ago, Bieksa opted to play provincial junior hockey until he was old enough to accept a scholarship offer to Bowling Green University starting in 2000. While majoring in finance, the defenceman was drafted by the Canucks after his freshman season, but he opted to stay in college until the end of his B.A. program.

Bieksa's rise was slow and methodical, starting with a few games with the Manitoba Moose in the spring of 2004, after he had graduated from Bowling Green. He played all of the next season with the AHL team, half the next year after with the Canucks, and then all of 2006–07 in the NHL, completing his development and maturation.

His career came to a halt during a game against Nashville on November 1, 2007, when he suffered a deep cut to the back of his right leg. The laceration required many stitches and kept him out of the lineup for more than half the season. He emerged as one of the team's best blue-liners the following year, though, but in 2009–10 he suffered another serious leg cut, this time to his left leg above the ankle, severing tendons and forcing him out of the lineup for some three months.

Meanwhile, his value to the team was evident every time he was on the ice, and in 2011 he became the hero in the Conference Final against San Jose. A fortuitous bounce saw him get the puck at the point in double overtime and beat Sharks goalie Antti Niemi with a quick shot to give the Canucks a 3–2 win in the game and a 4–1 win in the series, advancing the team to the Stanley Cup Final for the first time since 1994 and affording the players a much-needed one week break before game one.

Career Statistics	Regular Season					Playoffs				
	GP	G	A	P	Pim	GP	G	A	P	Pim
2005-06 VAN	39	0	6	6	77	DNQ				
2006-07 VAN	81	12	30	42	134	9	0	0	0	20
2007-08 VAN	34	2	10	12	90	DNQ				
2008-09 VAN	72	11	32	43	97	10	0	5	5	14
2009-10 VAN	55	3	19	22	85	12	3	5	8	14
2010-11 VAN	66	6	16	22	73	for 2011 playoff stats see p. 19				
NHL Totals	347	34	113	147	556					

for 2011 playoff stats see p. 19

Bolduc, Alexandre

b. Montreal, Quebec, June 26, 1985

Centre—shoots left

6'1" 197 lbs.

Drafted 127th overall by St. Louis in 2003

An unlikely path to the NHL if there ever was one, Bolduc didn't play his first NHL game until he was twenty-three years old in 2008, even though he had been drafted by St. Louis five-and-a-half years earlier.

He had been playing for Rouyn-Noranda in the QMJHL when the Blues acquired his rights, but after graduating from junior two years later he hadn't signed a contract and became a free agent. With no other NHL team interested in him, Bolduc signed with the Bakersfield Condors of the ECHL, hardly the route to take for NHL success. However, he played so well in that first season, 2005–06, that he began being called up to play for the Manitoba Moose, Vancouver's AHL affiliate.

This set up lasted two years before the Moose signed him full time for the 2007–08 season. Finally, after Bolduc played a full year in the AHL and acquitted himself well, the Canucks signed him to an NHL contract. He still played with the Moose for most of 2008–09, but he did get into seven NHL games as an emergency replacement for the injured Ryan Johnson.

In 2009–10, though, he missed most of the season with a serious shoulder injury, and he again split the 2010–11 season between the NHL and AHL. In the 2011 playoffs, though, he provided depth insurance for coach Alain Vigneault, and although he saw limited action, he contributed to the team's good fortune all the same.

Career Statistics	Regular Season					Playoffs				
	GP	G	A	P	Pim	GP	G	A	P	Pim
2008-09 VAN	7	0	1	1	4	DNP				
2009-10 VAN	15	0	0	0	13	DNP				
2010-11 VAN	24	2	2	4	21	for 2011 playoff stats see p. 19				
NHL Totals	46	2	3	5	38					

Burrows, Alexandre

b. Pincourt, Quebec, April 11, 1981

Left wing—shoots left

6'1" 188 lbs.

Undrafted

At a time when no one was interested in signing him, except pro hockey teams at the lowest level, Alexandre Burrows led a double life. In the winter he played hockey, but in the summers he played ball hockey, becoming, in fact, one of the most successful players in Canada's recent history. Indeed, he led Canada to World Championship gold in ball hockey in 2003 and 2005, and in 2010 he was inducted into the Canadian Ball Hockey Association Hall of Fame.

On ice, though, he wasn't having the same success. After two years with Shawinigan in the QMJHL, he went undrafted by the NHL and signed with Greenville of the ECHL. A "shift disturber," he was undisciplined and reviled by opponents and didn't make the most of his skills at this time. Over the course of the next three years, though, a large dose of hockey in the minors helped straighten him out, and the Canucks signed him to a two-way contract for 2005–06.

At first, Burrows made a reputation for himself through his penalty-killing and work as a fourth-liner with the Canucks, eventually teaming with Ryan Kesler on the third line and gaining extra ice time and greater responsibility. But early in the 2008–09 season, coach Alain Vigneault tried Burrows on the top line with Daniel and Henrik Sedin, and the combination worked. Burrows finished that year with twenty-eight goals, by far the highest total of his career.

The Sedins and Burrows were a force in 2009–10, leading the team's power play, Henrik captured the league's scoring title and Daniel wasn't far behind. Burrows responded in kind, scoring 35 goals and 67 points, shocking numbers given signs from early in his career. His totals included hat tricks in consecutive games, the first time in a quarter century a Canuck had achieved this feat.

Burrows's finest hour came in the opening round of the 2011 playoffs. The Canucks were cruising along, winning the first three games against Chicago, but the Hawks stormed back to tie the series and force game seven. The Canucks won that deciding game, 2–1 in overtime, with Burrows scoring both goals for the team. Vancouver both advanced to the second round and overcame the psychological demons which had seen the Hawks take out the Canucks from the playoffs in both 2010 and 2009.

Career Statistics	Regular Season					Playoffs				
	GP	G	A	P	Pim	GP	G	A	P	Pim
2005-06 VAN	43	7	5	12	61	DNQ				
2006-07 VAN	81	3	6	9	93	11	1	0	1	14
2007-08 VAN	82	12	19	31	179	DNQ				
2008-09 VAN	82	28	23	51	150	10	3	1	4	20
2009-10 VAN	82	35	32	67	121	12	3	3	6	22
2010-11 VAN	72	26	22	48	77	for 2011 playoff stats see p. 19				
NHL Totals	442	111	107	218	681					

for 2011 playoff stats see p. 19

Edler, Alexander

b. Ostersund, Sweden, April 21, 1986

Defence—shoots left

6'3" 215 lbs.

Drafted 91st overall by Vancouver in 2004

It was only by dint of Vancouver's European scout, Thomas Gradin, that the Canucks were able to draft Edler when they did in 2004. At the time, the defenceman was playing in Sweden for Jamtland, a third-tier team hardly worthy of scouting. But Edler's skating and control with the puck appeared so vastly superior to Gradin that he recommended the player with the highest marks.

Edler played one more year in Sweden with MoDo, a team located in Ornskoldsvik, perhaps the finest small city in the world (outside Canada) to produce hockey talent, with the Sedins, Markus Naslund, and Peter Forsberg among others, all hailing from there. The Canucks convinced Edler to play junior hockey in Canada the following year in nearby Kelowna, and at the end of that season he played at the U20 championship in Vancouver.

Although he was lower down on the depth charts, Edler played twenty-two games with the Canucks in 2006–07, largely because of injuries to other defencemen, but he acquitted himself well. Starting in 2007 he was a full-time player for the team, utilizing his skating and tremendous shot to his advantage, and earning extra time on the power play.

When the Canucks failed to make the playoffs in 2008, he accepted an invitation to play for Tre Kronor at the World Championship, and although the team lost the bronze-medal game, he was nonetheless impressive.

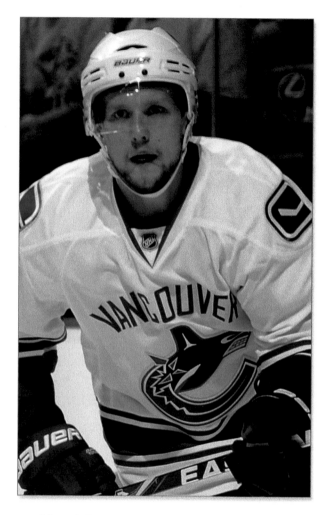

Although he is not a physical player, his offensive talent has made him one of the team's most valued assets, made even more so by the departure of his usual defensive partner and countryman, Mattias Ohlund, who left in 2009 as a free agent.

Career Statistics	Regular Season					Playoffs				
	GP	G	A	P	Pim	GP	G	A	P	Pim
2006-07 VAN	22	1	2	3	6	3	0	0	0	2
2007-08 VAN	75	8	12	20	42	DNQ				
2008-09 VAN	80	10	27	37	54	10	1	7	8	6
2009-10 VAN	76	5	37	42	40	12	2	4	6	10
2010-11 VAN	51	8	25	33	24	for 2011 playoff stats see p. 19				
NHL Totals	304	32	103	135	166					

Ehrhoff, Christian

b. Moers, West Germany (Germany), July 6, 1982

Defence—shoots left

6'2" 203 lbs.

Drafted 106th overall by San Jose in 2001

Although his boyhood idol was Bobby Orr, Christian Ehrhoff grew up in a part of the world in which few people knew that Orr was synonymous with great hockey. Yet, because of his excellent skating ability, he was able to distinguish himself while playing in the DEL, the top level of hockey in Germany, and San Jose drafted him in the summer of 2001 just before his nineteenth birthday.

Ehrhoff was cut at his first training camp that September but returned to Germany and kept working on his game. He played for Germany at the 2002 Olympics and the 2002 and 2003 World Championship and became a fine offensive defenceman, indeed.

Two years later, he came back to North America and has been here ever since. He spent most of his first two seasons with San Jose's AHL affiliate in Cleveland, but by 2006 he had proved to be an indispensable player to the big club. For the next three years he was a top blue-liner, getting more ice time and playing in more key situations. Not surprisingly, his scoring improved as well, but in the summer of 2009, the Sharks had to make salary cap space for the acquisition of Dany Heatley from Ottawa and decided to trade Ehrhoff.

The Canucks were willing takers, acquiring him and Brad Lukowich for Daniel Rahimi and Patrick White. Ehrhoff became an immediate hit with the Canucks, becoming truly a fine rushing defenceman who could also play in his own end with necessary responsibility.

In each of the last two seasons he had had career highs for goals (14) and bettered his best points as well, from 44 to 50.

In addition to his NHL career, Ehrhoff has now played at three Olympics, four World Championships, and the 2004 World Cup, becoming arguably the best defenceman Germany has ever produced, excepting the current national team coach, Uwe Krupp.

Career Statistics	Regular Season					Playoffs				
	GP	G	A	P	Pim	GP	G	A	P	Pim
2003-04 SJ	41	1	11	12	14	DNP				
2005-06 SJ	64	5	18	23	32	11	2	6	8	18
2006-07 SJ	82	10	23	33	63	11	0	2	2	6
2007-08 SJ	77	1	21	22	72	10	0	5	5	14
2008-09 SJ	77	8	34	42	63	6	0	0	0	2
2009-10 VAN	80	14	30	44	42	12	3	4	7	8
2010-11 VAN	79	14	36	50	52	for 2011 playoff stats see p. 19				
NHL Totals	500	53	173	226	338					

for 2011 playoff stats see p. 19

Glass, Tanner

b. Regina, Saskatchewan, November 29, 1983

Left wing—shoots left

6'1" 210 lbs.

Drafted 265th overall by Florida in 2003

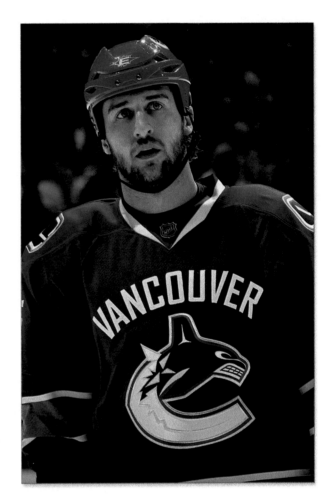

Another in a series of fairy-tale endings, Glass was one of the lowest drafted players ever to make the NHL. By no means a superstar, he has become an essential and effective fourth liner who can give a coach some much needed minutes on the ice, play hard defence, and check the other team's best players.

Glass played provincial hockey with Penticton and then went to Dartmouth College in 2003 on a four-year scholarship after being a low draft choice by Florida in the summer. He stayed for four years, being named captain of the Big Green for his senior year, and then he turned pro. He split his rookie season between Florida and the team's AHL affiliate in Rochester, but the year after he slipped on the depth chart and played only three games with the Panthers.

Glass became an unrestricted free agent in 2009 and signed with the Canucks who were looking for a fourth liner with some size. He played double-digit minutes many nights, something that happened only infrequently with Florida, and he established himself as a checking forward with more than a bit of defensive ability. His physical play has impressed Vancouver management, as has his ability to support teammates when the need has arisen.

Career Statistics	Regular Season					Playoffs				
	GP	G	A	P	Pim	GP	G	A	P	Pim
2007-08 FLA	41	1	1	2	39	DNQ				
2008-09 FLA	3	0	0	0	7	DNQ				
2009-10 VAN	67	4	7	11	115	4	0	0	0	0
2010-11 VAN	73	3	7	10	72	for 2011 playoff stats see p. 19				
NHL Totals	184	8	15	23	233					

for 2011 playoff stats see p. 19

Hamhuis, Dan

b. Smithers, B.C., December 13, 1982

Defence—shoots left

6'1" 209 lbs.

Drafted 12th overall by Nashville in 2001

One of the most important free-agent signings by the Canucks in recent years, Dan Hamhuis is a star defenceman, gifted offensively, strong in his own end, a puck carrier, shot blocker, and hitter. He can do it all, and after flying under the radar for six years in Nashville, he emerged this past season as a bona fide stud on the Canucks blue-line.

Hamhuis played four years of junior hockey with the Prince George Cougars and was drafted twelfth overall by Nashville after his third season, in 2001. Although he attended Predators' training camp that fall, coach Barry Trotz sent him back to the WHL and told him to work on his game. He did, and then some.

In his final year of junior, Hamhuis was the WHL player of the year and the CHL defenceman of the year, developing into a hard hitting, smooth skating defenceman. He played at the 2001 and 2002 U20 tournament for Canada, winning a bronze and silver medal, and played the entire 2002–03 season in Milwaukee, Nashville's AHL farm team.

A year later, Hamhuis was ready for the NHL. He immediately became

one of the team's top defencemen, but his progress was halted when the lockout cancelled the 2004–05 season. Nonetheless, it might have been a blessing in disguise. He went back to the AHL and was a dominant player, and his first year back with the Predators saw him increase his offence and become a greater force from the blue-line.

As a result, Nashville signed Hamhuis to a four-year contract in 2006, and despite the emergence of other key players, including defencemen Shea Weber and Ryan Suter, the team struggled to make headway in the playoffs. The upside to this was that he played for Canada at four consecutive World Championships, winning a bronze medal and two silver medals and drawing rave reviews for his play.

Hamhuis was to become a free agent in the summer of 2010. Anticipating his departure, the Predators traded his rights to Philadelphia, and the Flyers quickly to Pittsburgh. Neither team could sign him, so Hamhuis became an unrestricted free agent on July 1, 2010, and the Canucks signed him just hours later. He immediately agreed to a six-year, twenty-seven million dollar contract and has been an integral part of the team's incredible success in the 2011 playoffs. He never played less than twenty minutes in a game and peaked in game two against Nashville, playing nearly thirty-eight minutes of the game which went to double overtime.

Career Statistics	Regular Season					Playoffs				
	GP	G	A	P	Pim	GP	G	A	P	Pim
2003-04 NAS	80	7	19	26	57	6	0	2	2	6
2005-06 NAS	82	7	31	38	70	5	0	2	2	2
2006-07 NAS	81	6	14	20	66	5	0	1	1	2
2007-08 NAS	80	4	23	27	66	6	1	1	2	6
2008-09 NAS	82	3	23	26	67	DNQ				
2009-10 NAS	78	5	19	24	49	6	0	2	2	2
2010-11 VAN	64	6	17	23	34	for 2011 playoff stats see p. 19				
NHL Totals	547	38	146	184	409					

for 2011 playoff stats see p. 19

Hansen, Jannik

b. Herlev, Denmark, March 15, 1986

Right wing—shoots right

6'1" 195 lbs.

Drafted 287th overall by Vancouver in 2004

A long shot if ever there was one to make the NHL, Hansen grew up just outside Copenhagen in a country hardly known for producing hockey players. Nonetheless, he came from good stock as his father had played for the Danish national team in his day. Jannik had a little bit of size and strength, but he was one of the last players selected in the 2004 Entry Draft.

He played for Denmark at the U18 tournament in 2004 at the top level, and also played the previous two years in Division I. At the U20 level, he also played three times, never in the top division, but in 2005–06 he decided to make a serious effort to make the NHL and played for Portland in the WHL. He had a very successful season, and as a result the Canucks signed him to a three-year contract that allowed the team to start him in the AHL with the Manitoba Moose.

Hansen's development was slow and gradual, but it was noticeable every year. He played a little more in the NHL each year and a little less in the AHL, and in 2010–11 he didn't

see Manitoba at all, playing the full eighty-two games in the NHL and being able to say he was one of the few Danes to make the league.

He made his NHL debut during the 2007 playoffs, appearing in ten games and registering an assist, the first Dane to record a post-season point. In 2007–08, he was slowed by a broken thumb and later a concussion. The next year he played only a couple of games with the Moose but again missed a month with a broken finger, and the year after, again as a full-time NHLer, he broke his hand in a fight and missed five weeks.

During these years Hansen was made available to play in the World Championship. He played for Denmark three times at the top level, in 2005, 2006, and 2008. In each case the team realized its goal by avoiding relegation to the lower groups and is now a reliable member of the top division.

Hansen's greatest assets are his speed and responsible play. Not flashy, he isn't the kind of winger to go end-to-end with the puck, but he has good hands and is fast, a good third-liner who can kill penalties and give the coach minutes on ice without worry.

Now an established member of the Canucks, Hansen in twenty-five years old and a bona fide NHLer, something even the Canucks might not have guessed seven years ago when they drafted him 287th overall, the fifth-to-last choice that year.

Career Statistics	Regular Season					Playoffs				
	GP	G	A	P	Pim	GP	G	A	P	Pim
2006-07 VAN	DNP					10	0	1	1	4
2007-08 VAN	5	0	0	0	2	DNQ				
2008-09 VAN	55	6	15	21	37	2	0	0	0	0
2009-10 VAN	47	9	6	15	18	12	1	2	3	4
2010-11 VAN	82	9	20	29	32	for 2011 playoff stats see p. 19				
NHL Totals	189	24	41	65	89					

Higgins, Chris

b. Smithtown, New York, June 2, 1983

Left wing—shoots left

6' 205 lbs.

Drafted 14th overall by Montreal in 2002

Montreal's loss is Vancouver's gain in the case of Chris Higgins. Although the Habs drafted him midway through the first round nearly a decade ago, they felt he was expendable in the summer of 2009 when they included him in a package to acquire Scott Gomez from the New York Rangers. It proved to be the start of a four-team journey for Higgins over the next year and a half, but when he landed in Vancouver he came to a team that knew exactly what his role would be—and he thrived.

Even in his early teens, Higgins knew he wanted to play in the NHL. He attended Avon Old Farms, a prep school in Connecticut which emphasized hockey, and from there he went straight to Yale where he majored in political science. Although not a huge producer of NHLers, Yale played in the ECAC and was a high-profile university. Higgins was rookie of the year as a freshman, and that summer Montreal drafted him. After just one more year, he left school to join the Habs.

During his two years at Yale, Higgins also played for the U.S. at the U20 tournament, although the team finished a disappointing fifth and fourth.

Higgins spent his first two years of pro with the AHL team, the Hamilton Bulldogs, although he did get into two games just to see how much faster the pace was and to what level he had to reach before being able to call himself an NHL player. Once the lockout was over, he was a twenty-two-year-old who made Montreal at training camp in 2005. He seemed to develop at an impressive rate, reaching twenty-seven goals by his third year, but he would get no further and the Habs needed help offensively.

As a rookie, Higgins scored twenty-three goals and looked to be a ray of sunshine for the team, but early the next year he suffered a bad ankle sprain, missed almost a quarter of the season, yet still managed twenty-two goals. This led to his career-best third season, but a weak fourth season led to the trade with the Rangers.

Higgins had a poor half season on Broadway and was traded to the Flames at the deadline, and in the summer he decided to sign as a free agent with Florida. By the deadline of the 2010–11 season, with

the Panthers seemingly out of the playoffs, they traded several players, Higgins among them. He landed in Vancouver, a team playing the best hockey in its forty years of existence, and Higgins fit in perfectly. A power forward, he was both big and strong and skilled around the net, and he was a team player. He never took the bad penalties that drove coaches crazy, and he willingly blocked shots, won faceoffs, and did all the little things a winning team needs.

Career Statistics	Regular Season					Playoffs				
	GP	G	A	P	Pim	GP	G	A	P	Pim
2003-04 MON	2	0	0	0	0	DNP				
2005-06 MON	80	23	15	38	26	6	1	3	4	0
2006-07 MON	61	22	16	38	26	DNQ				
2007-08 MON	82	27	25	52	22	12	3	2	5	2
2008-09 MON	57	12	11	23	22	4	2	0	2	2
2009-10 NYR	55	6	8	14	32	--	--	--	--	--
2009-10 CAL	12	2	1	3	0	DNQ				
2010-11 FLA	48	11	12	23	10	--	--	--	--	--
2010-11 VAN	14	2	3	5	6	for 2011 playoff stats see p. 19				
NHL Totals	411	105	91	196	144					

for 2011 playoff stats see p. 19

Hodgson, Cody

b. Toronto, Ontario, February 18, 1990

Centre—shoots right

6' 185 lbs.

Drafted 10th overall by Vancouver in 2008

One of the youngest players on the team, Hodgson played only a few games with the Canucks during the regular season before assuming a more prominent role in the playoffs. Although he is only twenty-one years old, he has a past rich in success.

Hodgson played hockey from an early age with Matt Duchene, another of the best young players in the NHL, and later with future stars Jeff Skinner and Alex Pietrangelo, all of whom are from the Greater Toronto Area. In midget he played with Steve Stamkos and Michael del Zotto, but all along Hodgson was making a name for himself as a highly-skilled playmaker and stickhandler extraordinaire.

Deciding to play junior in the OHL, Hodgson played four years with the Brampton Battalion, becoming team captain. He was named the player of the year for all Canada in 2008–09, the same year he appeared for Canada in his first IIHF events. In 2008, he played at the U18 tournament and in 2009 at the U20. In both years Canada won gold, and Hodgson was a major contributor both times, recording twelve points in seven games of the U18 and then sixteen points in just six games of the 2009 U20 to lead all scorers.

The 2009–10 season was difficult for Hodgson. He suffered a back injury in the summer of 2009 while training, but the injury was misdiagnosed. He missed two months, came back but didn't feel right, and finally got a second and third opinion from doctors who discovered more serious damage that hadn't been treated properly for nearly a year. While the season was a writeoff for Hodgson and a setback in his development, he persevered and continued to train when he was allowed.

Making his NHL debut with Vancouver on February 1, 2011, after spending the season in Manitoba, Hodgson stayed only eight games before being returned to the minors. He continued to impress with the Moose, though, and was called up for the NHL playoffs where he earned some decent ice time in some games and learned about what it takes to battle every shift during the grind and demands of a Stanley Cup chase.

Healthy, young, and motivated, Hodgson might well be a key to the Canucks' fortunes for years to come.

Career Statistics	Regular Season					Playoffs				
	GP	G	A	P	Pim	GP	G	A	P	Pim
2010-11 VAN	8	1	1	2	0	for 2011 playoff stats see p. 19				

Kesler, Ryan

b. Livonia, Michigan, August 31, 1984

Centre—shoots right

6'2" 202 lbs.

Drafted 23rd overall by Vancouver in 2003

One of the most dominant forces on the Canucks, Ryan Kesler will look back at the 2010–11 season as his breakout year, the one where he went from an NHL player learning the game to one where he became a dominant and imposing force with his every shift.

He started his rise through the ranks in 2000 when he joined the U.S. National Team Development Program in Ann Arbor, Michigan, near his home in Livonia, the same hometown of his boyhood hero, Mike Modano. Kesler was a blossoming star with the NTDP and played at the 2002 U18 tournament for the U.S., helping the team win gold. In 2002, he went to Ohio State University on scholarship, but he stayed only one year because the Canucks drafted him in 2003 and his future was too bright to stay in college any longer.

Kesler split his first season between Manitoba and the Canucks and the year after, 2004–05, he was with the Moose the entire season during the lockout. That year was a blessing in disguise for him as he filled out physically, matured, and became a young star ready for the NHL. His first full season was more about showing promise than being a dominant force. He became a controversial figure in the summer of 2006 when the Philadelphia Flyers

signed the restricted free agent to an offer sheet of $1.9 million for one year. The Canucks matched the offer despite a quadrupling of his salary, but the moved has proved worthwhile.

Kesler developed into a great two-way player, someone with obvious size and skill around the enemy net, but also a star on defence. He was nominated for the Selke Trophy three times (2008, 2009, and this past year), and has proved to be both a power forward and a defensive stalwart, a unique combination, to say the least.

After that promising first year, Kesler suffered a hip injury that kept him out of the lineup for half a year in 2006–07. He rebounded, though, and produced three straight years of twenty goals or more at a time when the Canucks were in desperate need of scoring. In the summer of 2007, the team lost Trevor Linden, Markus Naslund, and Brendan Morrison, so Kesler was given a greater role with the team—and he responded.

But even the Canucks weren't necessarily ready for his 2010–11 season. In eighty-two games, he had forty-one goals and proved a dominant force to spell the Sedin twins from having to deliver most of the offence. The result, of course, was a more potent lineup, game in, game out.

Kesler has also played at every level of international hockey for the U.S. In addition to those early U18 and U20 events, he played at the 2006 World Championship and last year helped the Americans to a silver medal at the Olympics. Still only twenty-six years of age and entering his prime, Kesler's best years might still be ahead of him.

Career Statistics	Regular Season					Playoffs				
	GP	G	A	P	Pim	GP	G	A	P	Pim
2003-04 VAN	28	2	3	5	16	DNP				
2005-06 VAN	82	10	13	23	79	DNQ				
2006-07 VAN	48	6	10	16	40	1	0	0	0	0
2007-08 VAN	80	21	16	37	79	DNQ				
2008-09 VAN	82	26	33	59	61	10	2	2	4	14
2009-10 VAN	82	25	50	75	104	12	1	9	10	4
2010-11 VAN	82	41	32	73	66	for 2011 playoff stats see p. 19				
NHL Totals	484	131	157	288	445					

for 2011 playoff stats see p. 19

Lapierre, Maxim

b. St. Leonard, Quebec, March 29, 1985

Centre—shoots right

6'2" 207 lbs.

Drafted 61th overall by Montreal in 2003

Although his style of play is not to everyone's liking, Maxim Lapierre wouldn't have it any other way. In the tradition of all good "pests," he is welcomed by his teammates and reviled by the opposition.

Lapierre started out in the QMJHL, playing four years and developing his skills as a player and agitator. He played for the short-lived Montreal Rocket from 2001 to 2003, before failing attendance forced the team to relocate to Prince Edward Island. Lapierre was drafted by the Canadiens during the transfer year, 2003, but he stayed in junior two full years longer until he was no longer eligible.

The next three years were years of maturation for the centreman. He played most of his first season with the team's AHL affiliate in Hamilton, but he did play in one NHL game, on November 15, 2005. The next year, he split time evenly between the NHL and AHL, and in 2007–08 he was mostly in the NHL. In the spring of 2007, the Canadiens didn't qualify for the playoffs but the Bulldogs did, so Lapierre was sent back to the farm and helped his team win the Calder Cup.

By training camp in 2008, the Habs decided they would keep him for the season, but his production the next year was cut in half and early in the 2010–11 season the Habs decided to make some changes. Montreal traded him to Anaheim for Brett Festerling and a draft choice, but that stint with the Ducks lasted only twenty-one games before the Canucks acquired him at the trade deadline.

Again, this was a case of Vancouver general manager Mike Gillis acquiring a specific player for a specific need, looking ahead to the playoffs. In the 2011 post-season Lapierre was playing almost a third of every game, was defensively responsible, and stayed out of the penalty box. He was an excellent penalty killer and was an added element that helped take the Canucks to within one win of the Stanley Cup.

Career Statistics	Regular Season					Playoffs				
	GP	G	A	P	Pim	GP	G	A	P	Pim
2005-06 MON	1	0	0	0	0	DNP				
2006-07 MON	46	6	6	12	24	DNQ				
2007-08 MON	53	7	11	18	60	12	0	3	3	6
2008-09 MON	79	15	13	28	76	4	0	0	0	26
2009-10 MON	76	7	7	14	61	19	3	1	4	20
2010-11 MON	38	5	3	8	63	--	--	--	--	--
2010-11 ANA	21	0	3	3	9	--	--	--	--	--
2010-11 VAN	19	1	0	1	8	for 2011 playoff stats see p. 19				
NHL Totals	333	41	43	84	301					

for 2011 playoff stats see p. 19

Luongo, Roberto

b. Montreal, Quebec, April 4, 1979

Goalie—catches left

6'3" 217 lbs.

Drafted 4th overall by NY Islanders in 1997

They call him "Bobby Loo" in Vancouver, the nickname a sign of how much fans and teammates in Vancouver love the big goalie who has been the number-one man in the blue ice since 2006. Luongo was drafted a lofty fourth overall in 1997, but his first days with the Islanders seem like a long time ago from his Cup-winning season of 2010–11.

Luongo was the future for the Islanders, but general manager Mike Milbury liked Rick DiPietro even more and selected him first overall in 2000, trading Luongo to Florida just before the draft. Luongo played five years with the Panthers during which time two things stood out. First, he became known as the goalie who faced more shots every year than any other goalie in the league, the result of the Panthers being a weak team and Luongo playing in an overwhelming majority of the team's games. And second, because the team never made the playoffs during his time there, Luongo often played for Canada at the World Championship. This is where he established his reputation as

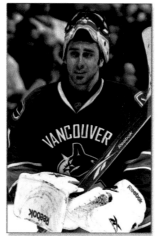

a winner, leading Canada to gold in 2003 and 2004, and winning a silver in 2005.

Luongo was acquired by the Canucks in the summer of 2006 in a blockbuster deal involving six players, the most prominent name going to Florida being Todd Bertuzzi, who had worn out his welcome in Vancouver. Luongo was coming to a team that, in recent years, was full of promise but often light on strong playoff goaltending. During his first four years, the team improved and added the necessary ingredients to a Cup-winning formula, but again playoff results were always just a little disappointing.

Luongo reached new heights of fame and confidence at the 2010 Olympics when he led Canada to Olympic gold. He started the event as the backup to Martin Brodeur, but Brodeur looked particularly vulnerable in a preliminary round 5–3 loss to the U.S. and coach Mike Babcock decided to give Luongo a chance. He seized the moment and played the rest of the way.

That confidence continued through Luongo's play with the Canucks, and combined with an ever-better defence, the team's back end never looked as impenetrable as during the 2011 playoffs. "Bobby Loo" started in Long Island on a bad team and worked his way up to the Stanley Cup Final, coming tantalizingly close to joining the Triple Gold Club in the process.

Career Statistics		Regular Season						Playoffs					
	GP	W-L-T-O/T	Mins	GA	SO	GAA		GP	W-L	Mins	GA	SO	GAA
1999-00 NYI	24	7-14-1-1	1,292	70	1	3.25		DNQ					
2000-01 FLA	47	12-24-7-5	2,628	107	5	2.44		DNQ					
2001-02 FLA	58	16-33-4-4	3,030	140	4	2.77		DNQ					
2002-03 FLA	65	20-34-7-6	3,627	164	6	2.71		DNQ					
2003-04 FLA	72	25-33-14-7	4,252	172	7	2.43		DNQ					
2005-06 FLA	75	35-30-0-9	4,305	213	4	2.97		DNQ					
2006-07 VAN	76	47-22-0-6	4,490	171	5	2.29		12	5-7	847	25	0	1.77
2007-08 VAN	73	35-29-0-9	4,233	168	6	2.38		DNQ					
2008-09 VAN	54	33-13-0-7	3,181	124	9	2.34		10	6-4	618	26	1	2.52
2009-10 VAN	68	40-22-0-4	3,899	167	4	2.57		12	6-6	707	38	0	3.22
2010-11 VAN	60	38-15-0-7	3,590	126	4	2.11		for 2011 playoff stats see p. 19					

for 2011 playoff stats see p. 19

Malhotra, Manny

b. Mississauga, Ontario, May 18, 1980

Centre—shoots left

6'2" 220 lbs.

Drafted 7th overall by NY Rangers in 1998

One of the top-ranked juniors when he started in the NHL in 1998, Malhotra has seen his role change over a decade and more in the league, but he is still a valuable team player, a fine checker, and an expert on faceoffs.

Twice he played for Canada at the U20 tournament, in 1998 and again in 2000, winning a bronze medal in the latter, but he never established himself with the Rangers the way the team had expected. As well, the Rangers were in a post-Gretzky building stage and never made the playoffs during Malhotra's time, and they traded him midway through his fourth season.

Unfortunately, the pattern repeated itself in Dallas, but when he was traded again, to Columbus, he was with a young team and little pressure. As a result, he enjoyed some fine seasons and bolstered his reputation, finding his niche as a checker and third-liner more suitable than the first-line superstar status he had as an eighteen-year-old.

The Blue Jackets were also a weak team that had trouble making the playoffs, though, so when the Sharks wooed him in the summer of 2009, he was interested. He signed a one-year deal, but at the end of the season he parted ways with the Sharks to join Vancouver. It was not a difficult decision for him. The Canucks presented him with a three-year contract worth $7.5 million—and a no-trade clause.

Malhotra's 2010–11 season seemed to come to an end in a game on March 16, 2011. He was hit in the eye by a puck in a game against Colorado and had surgery the next day. The extent of the problem was worse than expected and he needed a second procedure a few days later, and while it went well, doctors told him his season was done.

But hockey players heal at a remarkable rate, and just two months later he was skating lightly again. On May 29, with the Canucks now in the Stanley Cup Final, doctors cleared him for game action after he had participated in full-contact workouts. His recovery was nothing short of incredible, and Malhotra dressed in the Stanley Cup Final against the Bruins wearing a full shield, his season coming to a happy conclusion playing for the Stanley Cup, despite falling one game short.

Career Statistics	Regular Season					Playoffs				
	GP	G	A	P	Pim	GP	G	A	P	Pim
1998-99 NYR	73	8	8	16	13	DNQ				
1999-00 NYR	27	0	0	0	4	DNQ				
2000-01 NYR	50	4	8	12	31	DNQ				
2001-02 NYR	56	7	6	13	42	--	--	--	--	--
2001-02 DAL	16	1	0	1	5	DNQ				
2002-03 DAL	59	3	7	10	42	5	1	0	1	0
2003-04 DAL	9	0	0	0	4	--	--	--	--	--
2003-04 CBJ	56	12	13	25	24	DNQ				
2005-06 CBJ	58	10	21	31	41	DNQ				
2006-07 CBJ	82	9	16	25	76	DNQ				
2007-08 CBJ	71	11	18	29	34	DNQ				
2008-09 CBJ	77	11	24	35	28	4	0	0	0	0
2009-10 SJ	71	14	19	33	41	15	1	0	1	0
2010-11 VAN	72	11	19	30	22	for 2011 playoff stats see p. 19				
NHL Totals	777	101	159	260	407					

Oreskovich, Victor

b. Whitby, Ontario, August 15, 1986

Right wing—shoots right

6'3" 215 lbs.

Drafted 55th overall by Colorado in 2004

The path to a career in the NHL is not always straight and obvious. Victor Oreskovich is a case in point. Growing up in the Toronto area, he was obsessed with hockey as a kid and became very good at it. He was drafted by Windsor to play in the OHL, but instead of jumping into junior hockey right away he decided to spend a year in the USHL and consider his options. In the end, he decided to accept a scholarship offer from the University of Notre Dame and it was there he went in the fall of 2004 after being drafted by Colorado earlier in the summer.

Oreskovich was unhappy, though, as he didn't get as much playing time as he would have hoped and felt his development was stalling. Like a growing number of Canadians, he gave up on the NCAA and returned to junior back home, in his case joining Kitchener, which had acquired his rights.

After half a season with the OHL's Kitchener Rangers, Oreskovich attended the Avalanche's training camp in 2007, but was an early cut. He was assigned to the farm team in Lake Erie but decided not to report. The team suspended him, and he promptly retired from the game at age nineteen, citing mental fatigue and lack of dedication to the game.

That seemed to be the end for Oreskovich, but two years later he re-discovered his love for the game. Florida signed him as a free agent, and he was assigned to the AHL team in Rochester where he played well. The Panthers called him up mid-season, and he remained in the NHL the rest of the year, playing well, indeed.

On draft day 2010, though, the Panthers traded him to the Canucks in a big deal which saw Keith Ballard and Steve Bernier join him in Vancouver while the Panthers got Michael Grabner and a first-round draft choice. Oreskovich started 2010–11 with Manitoba, but he was called up in February and has been with the Canucks ever since.

Career Statistics	Regular Season					Playoffs				
	GP	G	A	P	Pim	GP	G	A	P	Pim
2009-10 FLA	50	2	4	6	26	DNQ				
2010-11 VAN	16	0	3	3	8	for 2011 playoff stats see p. 19				
NHL Totals	66	2	7	9	34					

Rome, Aaron

b. Nesbitt, Manitoba, September 27, 1983

Defence—shoots left

6'1" 218 lbs.

Drafted 104th overall by Los Angeles in 2002

One of four hockey-playing brothers from a town in Manitoba with a population of thirty, Aaron Rome is the only sibling to have made it as far as the NHL. Ashton was drafted in 2006 by San Jose while Ryan and Reagan have played minor pro.

Aaron had a unique junior career in the WHL in that he played for four teams between 1998 and 2004. Although he was drafted by the L.A. Kings in 2002, he never signed a contract in the ensuing two years and as a result became a free agent. The Ducks signed him in 2004, and for the next three years he played in their system.

Rome's first two years, 2004–06, passed entirely in the minors, but he did get into two NHL games the following season. He made his debut on January 2, 2007, and he later played in one playoff game. That game was not in the Stanley Cup Final, though, so even though the Ducks won their first Cup, Rome didn't get his name on the Cup. (He did get a ring and his day with the trophy in the summer, though.)

Early the next season the Ducks traded Rome to Columbus with Clay Wilson for Geoff Platt, and he was assigned to the Blue Jackets' farm team in Syracuse. He spent the next two seasons with Columbus, appearing in only twenty-five regular-season games and one more in the playoffs. In the summer of 2009 he decided to sign with Vancouver because the Canucks were willing to give him a one-way contract, a sign of good faith that he was going to play in the NHL and

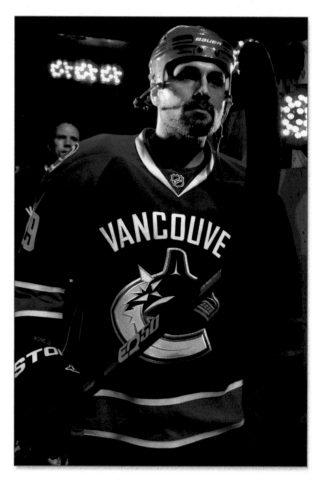

Sure enough, Rome played only a few games with Manitoba in 2009–10 and none at all in 2010–11. A third- or fourth-liner who has a physical edge to his play, Rome started off the 2011 playoffs by taking a regular shift, although he was sometimes a healthy scratch for Alain Vigneault, who tailored his lineup to what the opposition featured.

Career Statistics	Regular Season					Playoffs				
	GP	G	A	P	Pim	GP	G	A	P	Pim
2006-07 ANA	1	0	0	0	0	1	0	0	0	0
2007-08 CBJ	17	1	1	2	33	DNQ				
2008-09 CBJ	8	0	1	1	0	1	0	1	1	0
2009-10 VAN	49	0	4	4	24	1	0	0	0	0
2010-11 VAN	56	1	4	5	53	for 2011 playoff stats see p. 19				
NHL Totals	131	2	10	12	110					

Raymond, Mason

VANCOUVER

b. Cochrane, Alberta, September 17, 1985

Left wing—shoots left

6' 185 lbs.

Drafted 51th overall by Vancouver in 2005

An outstanding skater with offensive skills, Mason Raymond has worked his way into the Vancouver lineup and become an instrumental part of the team. He began in provincial junior hockey, thinking about a college career when he started playing for the Camrose Kodiaks in 2003. At the end of his second year he was named the Alberta Junior Hockey League's MVP, and just a few weeks later the Canucks drafted him.

Raymond attended the University of Minnesota-Duluth for two years and towards the end of his second season he was called up to play a few games with the Canucks' farm team, Manitoba Moose. Raymond decided to forego his final two years of NCAA eligibility to turn pro, and in 2007 he was assigned to the Moose at Vancouver's main training camp.

After a strong start in the NHL, playing on a line with the Sedins, Raymond was demoted but later called up when injuries depleted the lineup. He took advantage of the opportunity but was up and down for much of the season. Not so in 2008–09. Raymond didn't play at all in the minors, was invited to participate in the YoungStars Game during the NHL's All-Star Weekend in Montreal, and has taken on an evermore prominent role with the team.

In 2009–10, Raymond had a career year with twenty-five goals and finished the season playing for Canada at the World Championship. That summer he avoided arbitration by signing a two-year contract with the Canucks, and although he had only fifteen goals this past season he did enough things well to ensure his place in the lineup throughout the 2011 playoffs, rising to the occasion until being knocked out with an injury in game six of the final.

Career Statistics	Regular Season					Playoffs				
	GP	G	A	P	Pim	GP	G	A	P	Pim
2007-08 VAN	49	9	12	21	2	DNQ				
2008-09 VAN	72	11	12	23	24	10	2	1	3	2
2009-10 VAN	82	25	28	53	48	12	3	1	4	6
2010-11 VAN	70	15	24	39	10	for 2011 playoff stats see p. 19				
NHL Totals	273	60	76	136	84					

for 2011 playoff stats see p. 19

Salo, Sami

b. Turku, Finland, September 2, 1974

Defence—shoots right

6'3" 212 lbs.

Drafted 239th overall by Ottawa in 1996

An incredible athlete and the oldest player on the Canucks, Salo is well regarded both as an excellent defenceman and for his superhuman ability to overcome injury. The thirty-seven-year-old has a resume of missed games for every reason imaginable that rivals the scoring statistics of his long and industrious career.

A very low draft choice by Ottawa in 1996, both team and player felt there was no reason to rush his development, so he stayed in Finland until he was twenty-four years old, playing for TPS and Jokerit. But in 1998, he came over to Canada and impressed the Senators enough that they decided to keep him for most of the year. Salo displayed great skating ability, a terrific shot, and hard-nosed physical play inside his own blue-line. In short, he could do it all, except he lacked experience at this time.

Salo played for the Senators for four years. Although they made it to

the playoffs every year they, didn't ever get past the second round. Nevertheless, he logged more than twenty minutes of ice time a game and was always a plus player in the plus-minus stats, and it was clear he was a top defenceman.

The Senators decided to trade him on September 21, 2002, to Vancouver for Peter Schaefer, and he has been with the Canucks ever since. Salo is both an anchor on the power play and a defenceman who can play against the other team's top line. His only weakness is a propensity for injury. Over the years he has missed games because of injuries to his shoulder, knee, and foot. He has suffered a concussion, had teeth knocked out, suffered from a bad case of the flu, back spasms, and a broken finger. He hurt another shoulder, suffered nerve damage, fractured his wrist, and broken a rib. He even missed two games after being bitten by a snake.

Salo has also had an extraordinary career internationally. He first played for Finland at the 2001 World Championship, winning a silver medal, and in 2004 he played at both the Worlds and the World Cup of Hockey. He has also played at three Olympics for Finland, winning a silver medal in 2006 and bronze in 2010.

Career Statistics	Regular Season					Playoffs				
	GP	G	A	P	Pim	GP	G	A	P	Pim
1998-99 OTT	61	7	12	19	24	4	0	0	0	0
1999-00 OTT	37	6	8	14	2	6	1	1	2	0
2000-01 OTT	31	2	16	18	10	4	0	0	0	0
2001-02 OTT	66	4	14	18	14	12	2	1	3	4
2002-03 VAN	79	9	21	30	10	12	1	3	4	0
2003-04 VAN	74	7	19	26	22	7	1	2	3	2
2005-06 VAN	59	10	23	33	38	DNQ				
2006-07 VAN	67	14	23	37	26	10	0	1	1	4
2007-08 VAN	63	8	17	25	38	DNQ				
2008-09 VAN	60	5	20	25	26	7	3	4	7	2
2009-10 VAN	68	9	19	28	18	12	1	5	6	2
2010-11 VAN	27	3	4	7	14	for 2011 playoff stats see p. 19				
NHL Totals	692	84	196	280	242					

for 2011 playoff stats see p. 19

Samuelsson, Mikael

b. Mariefred, Sweden, December 23, 1976

Right wing—shoots right

6'2" 218 lbs.

Drafted 145th overall by San Jose in 1998

A low draft choice from Sweden, Samuelsson was *not* selected by the Detroit Red Wings like so many others who fit the bill. Not surprisingly, however, he ended up with the Wings, but this was one player Detroit regrets losing to free agency. Mikael Samuelsson not only does it all, he possesses that one golden quality that cannot be explained, only identified. He is a winner.

He wasn't drafted until he was twenty-two years old while he was playing in the Swedish Elite League, and it was there he stayed another two years before deciding to give the NHL a chance. Samuelsson attended San Jose's training camp in the fall of 2000 but was soon sent to the team's minor-league affiliate in Kentucky.

The next two years were a mish-mash of uncertainty, injury, and minimal opportunity for Samuelsson. He split 2002–03 between the Rangers and Pittsburgh, and another trade sent him to Florida for the following season, one which saw him miss long stretches with a broken jaw and hand. During the lockout he returned to Sweden and helped Sodertalje win the SEL championship, and late in the summer of 2005, he signed a contract with Detroit, marking a change in the direction of his career.

The Red Wings saw Samuelsson as a strong forward with a great shot and an asset to the team's offense. They never had him in the minors, played him on the second or third line, and watched him thrive. In 2005–06, he also made international history. Samuelsson was named to the Olympic team for Sweden and won gold, and after the Red Wings were eliminated in the first round of the playoffs he ended the season playing for Tre Kronor at the World Championship. He won another gold there, one of only eight players from both gold teams that year and the first players to win the golden double.

Two years later, he was instrumental in the Red Wings winning the Stanley Cup, joining the Triple Gold Club in the process. But the Red Wings took Samuelsson's place on the team too lightly, and they didn't make vigorous efforts to re-sign him until after the Canucks made an impressive offer in the summer of 2009. Samuelsson signed with Vancouver, ending his successful, four-year career in Detroit.

Of course, Vancouver knew the player it was getting, but Samuelsson was especially motivated to prove the Red Wings wrong, and to the rest of the league that he was a superstar. He scored thirty goals and was perhaps the team's best player in the 2010 playoffs. He was having an inconsistent 2011 playoffs, though, playing through injury, when he suffered a more serious injury in a game against Nashville in the second round of the playoffs. He had to have surgery to repair a sports hernia and missed the rest of the playoffs.

Career Statistics	Regular Season					Playoffs				
	GP	G	A	P	Pim	GP	G	A	P	Pim
2000-01 SJ	4	0	0	0	0	DNP				
2001-02 NYR	67	6	10	16	23	DNQ				
2002-03 NYR	58	8	14	22	32	--	--	--	--	--
2002-03 PIT	22	2	0	2	8	DNQ				
2003-04 FLA	37	3	6	9	35	DNQ				
2005-06 DET	71	23	22	45	42	6	0	1	1	0
2006-07 DET	53	14	20	34	28	18	3	8	11	14
2007-08 DET	73	11	29	40	26	22	5	8	13	8
2008-09 DET	81	19	21	40	50	23	5	5	10	6
2009-10 VAN	74	30	23	53	64	12	8	7	15	16
2010-11 VAN	75	18	32	50	36	for 2011 playoff stats see p. 19				
NHL Totals	615	134	177	311	344					

Schneider, Cory

b. Marblehead, Massachusetts, March 18, 1986

Goalie—catches left

6'2" 195 lbs.

Drafted 26th overall by Vancouver in 2004

In years past there has been little consolation in being named backup to Roberto Luongo. Luongo, a workaholic, often plays seventy games or more in a season, so his backup is likely to see little game action over the course of a season. But Schneider broke that pattern in 2010–11 and did so after displaying patience ever since the Canucks drafted him seven years ago.

In 2004, he had just finished a year with the U.S. National Team Development Program where he helped the team win a silver medal at the 2004 U18 tournament. He had an outstanding tournament, winning five of six games and posting a 1.71 GAA. Schneider then went to Boston College for three years, splitting the goaltending chores in his first year and becoming the number-one man in years two and three. He was an exceptional goalie for Boston College in Hockey East, and he also played for USA Hockey at two U20 tournaments, finishing fourth both times.

In 2007, he decided to turn pro and join the Canucks. They assigned him to Manitoba for all of 2007–08, after which it became clear he might well be the team's second-best goalie for the NHL.

But the Canucks always seemed to have another backup in mind, from Curtis Sanford to Andrew Raycroft. Still, Schneider kept playing well whenever he got the chance. He was called up for eight games in 2008–09 when Luongo was injured, but only played two in 2010–11. Schneider was named the AHL's best goalie in 2008–09 despite playing only forty games, and he took the team to the Calder Cup finals before losing to Hershey in six games.

His break came in 2010–11 when Luongo was again sidelined and coach Alain Vigneault gave him a chance to play even more. Schneider responded with excellent goaltending, and soon he was the clear number-two goalie. Indeed, Vigneault got him into enough games to ensure that he shared honours with Luongo when the Canucks won the William Jennings Trophy for fewest goals allowed in the regular season.

Career Statistics			Regular Season				Playoffs					
	GP	W-L-O	Mins	GA	SO	GAA	GP	W-L	Mins	GA	SO	GAA
2008-09 VAN	8	2-4-1	355	20	0	3.38	DNP					
2009-10 VAN	2	0-1-0	79	5	0	3.80	DNP					
2010-11 VAN	25	16-4-2	1,372	51	1	2.23	for 2011 playoff stats see p. 19					
NHL Totals	35	18-9-3	1,806	76	1	2.53						

for 2011 playoff stats see p. 19

Sedin, Daniel

b. Ornskoldsvik, Sweden, September 26, 1980

Left wing—shoots left

6'1" 187 lbs.

Drafted 2nd overall by Vancouver in 1999

Daniel is six minutes younger than his twin brother, Henrik, and he is the goal scorer while Henrik is the passer. These are about the only ways to tell the two apart, that and the fact that Daniel wears 22 and Henrik wears 33.

The brothers were born in Ornskoldsvik, a small town in northern Sweden which is also the birthplace of Peter Forsberg and Markus Naslund. Such is their one-ness that even while playing in Sweden with MoDo, they were named co-MVPs of the league in 1998–99, their final year before the NHL draft. That was a strange time for the NHL because it was clear the brothers wanted to play together and any team would want them as a pair because they made each other play better.

On draft morning, Vancouver general manager Brian Burke declared that he wasn't leaving the draft without the pair, and through swift and shrewd negotiations he got his way. He selected Daniel second and Henrik third, stealing the thunder of the draft from all other teams.

The brothers decided to play another year in MoDo before joining the Canucks for the 2000–01 season. In truth, they didn't exactly take the NHL by storm.

Their forte was cycling the puck to create an open man, moving the puck along the boards, darting and turning one way and then another before springing a man loose. But when they first got to the NHL, they were not so physically strong that they were effective at cycling. Daniel had twenty goals and thirty-four points as a rookie, but the team lost in four straight games in the opening round of the playoffs.

Daniel's next three seasons were all a little disappointing based on the high draft choices used for the brothers. They looked like they were just around the corner from superstardom, but that corner didn't come. Not just yet, anyway.

In some respects the brothers took their final step to maturity during the NHL lockout of 2004–05. They returned home and played the year for MoDo and then went to the World Championship, and when they got back to Vancouver for 2005–06, they were different players. Daniel set career highs for goals and points in that season and became something of a leader on the team. He was now twenty-five years old and entering his prime years.

Indeed, ever since then he has not just been a rising star or a top player on the team but one of the best players in the NHL. In the last five years, he has averaged thirty-three goals a season and nearly a point a game in the playoffs as well. Of course, he reached the peak of his career to date in 2010–11 by winning the Art Ross Trophy, the only player in the league to reach the 100-point mark during the regular season.

Career Statistics	Regular Season					Playoffs				
	GP	G	A	P	Pim	GP	G	A	P	Pim
2000-01 VAN	75	20	14	34	24	4	1	2	3	0
2001-02 VAN	79	9	23	32	32	6	0	1	1	0
2002-03 VAN	79	14	17	31	34	14	1	5	6	8
2003-04 VAN	82	18	36	54	18	7	1	2	3	0
2005-06 VAN	82	22	49	71	34	DNQ				
2006-07 VAN	81	36	48	84	16	12	2	3	5	4
2007-08 VAN	82	29	45	74	50	DNQ				
2008-09 VAN	82	31	51	82	36	10	4	6	10	8
2009-10 VAN	63	29	56	85	28	12	5	9	14	12
2010-11 VAN	82	41	63	104	32	for 2011 playoff stats see p. 19				
NHL Totals	787	249	402	651	324					

Sedin, Henrik

b. Ornskoldsvik, Sweden, September 26, 1980

Centre—shoots left

6'2" 188 lbs.

Drafted 3rd overall by Vancouver in 1999

When Henrik won the Art Ross Trophy in 2009–10, he had just twenty-nine goals. No player had led the league in scoring with fewer goals since 1949–50 when Ted Lindsay had twenty-three. Joe Thornton and Peter Forsberg had also won with twenty-nine, and in all cases these were players who were known as passers first, shooters second. Henrik's talents came about naturally because he played most of his life with brother Daniel, a more natural scorer. It would only make sense his brother would be a passer then.

What is more incredible is how close the twins are in scoring. Over the course of 10 NHL seasons, Henrik has averaged .822 points per game while Daniel has averaged .827 points per game, an infinitesimal difference! The similarities extend to international hockey. Daniel had 25 points in three career U20 tournaments while Henrik had 26. Both played 20 games. At the Olympics, they both played 12 games, Daniel with 7 points, Henrik with 6. At the World Championship, Daniel had

17 points in 28 games and Henrik has 12 points in 33 games. The difference in games played came as a result of 2001 when Daniel suffered a back injury and played only three of nine games.

Henrik increased his point totals every year for the first six years of his NHL career, and like Daniel, he took his game to a new level after the lockout, starting in 2005–06. The brothers also made NHL history over the last two seasons, when each won the Art Ross Trophy in consecutive seasons, becoming the first brothers to do so. Doug and Max Bentley won in the 1940s, but their wins were three years apart. The Sedins are also only the fifth set of twins to play after Chris and Peter Ferraro, Joel and Henrik Lundqvist, Rich and Ron Sutter, and Peter and Patrik Sundstrom.

In addition to their NHL careers, the brothers have had success for Tre Kronor, most significantly in 2006 when they helped their country win gold at the Olympics in Turin. They have won two bronze medals at the World Championship, though they decided not to play in 2006 after the Olympics and missing the playoffs, deciding rest was more important. But their long and consistent devotion to Sweden in international play cannot be over-stated as they first played for their country at the 1998 U20 tournament and many more since.

Career Statistics	Regular Season					Playoffs				
	GP	G	A	P	Pim	GP	G	A	P	Pim
2000-01 VAN	82	9	20	29	38	4	0	4	4	0
2001-02 VAN	82	16	20	36	36	6	3	0	3	0
2002-03 VAN	78	8	31	39	38	14	3	2	5	8
2003-04 VAN	76	11	31	42	32	7	2	2	4	2
2005-06 VAN	82	18	57	75	56	DNQ				
2006-07 VAN	82	10	71	81	66	12	2	2	4	14
2007-08 VAN	82	15	61	76	56	DNQ				
2008-09 VAN	82	22	60	82	48	10	4	6	10	2
2009-10 VAN	82	29	83	112	48	12	3	11	14	6
2010-11 VAN	82	19	75	94	40	for 2011 playoff stats see p. 19				
NHL Totals	810	157	509	666	458					

Tambellini, Jeff

b. Calgary, Alberta, April 13, 1984

Left wing—shoots left

5'11" 186 lbs.

Drafted 27th overall by Los Angeles in 2003

The third generation of a very successful hockey family, Jeff has had some big skates to fill. His grandfather, Addie Tambellini, was part of the Trail Smoke Eaters team that won gold for Canada at the 1961 World Championship. His father, Steve Tambellini, had a ten-year NHL career that culminated in 1989 when he helped the Calgary Flames win the Stanley Cup. If only Jeff could win Olympic gold, the Tambellinis would be the first Triple Gold Club family!

In part because of his pedigree, and in larger measure because he had an outstanding NCAA career, Jeff was a first-round draft choice by Los Angeles in 2003. He had played provincial junior hockey in his home province of British Columbia before going to the University of Michigan under legendary head coach Red Berenson, and with the Wolverines he became a more important part of the team every year. During his NCAA days, he also played for Canada at the 2004 U20 tournament, winning a silver medal.

Tambellini played three years at U of M before turning pro with the Kings, spending most of 2005–06 with the farm team in Manchester. He did get into four games with the Kings, but late in the season he was traded to the Islanders. He finished the season in the NHL but spent most of the next four years bouncing between the NHL and the Bridgeport Sound Tigers of the AHL.

The 2009–10 season was particularly frustrating for him. Although he didn't play in the minors and was injury-free, he appeared in only thirty-six games, often being relegated to the press box as a healthy scratch. As a result, it wasn't difficult for him to leave the Islanders in the summer of 2010 when he became a free agent, and when his home province Canucks expressed an interest in signing him, it was easy for him to change teams.

Although he played briefly in the farm system with Manitoba this past season, Tambellini has made a decent contribution with the Canucks and he saw only limited action in the 2011 playoffs.

Career Statistics	Regular Season					Playoffs				
	GP	G	A	P	Pim	GP	G	A	P	Pim
2005-06 LA	4	0	0	0	2	--	--	--	--	--
2005-06 NYI	21	1	3	4	8	DNQ				
2006-07 NYI	23	2	7	9	6	DNP				
2007-08 NYI	31	1	3	4	8	DNQ				
2008-09 NYI	65	7	8	15	32	DNQ				
2009-10 NYI	36	7	7	14	14	DNQ				
2010-11 VAN	62	9	8	17	18	for 2011 playoff stats see p. 19				
NHL Totals	242	27	36	63	88					

for 2011 playoff stats see p. 19

Tanev, Chris

b. Toronto, Ontario, December 20, 1989
Defence—shoots right
6'2" 185 lbs.
Undrafted

The twenty-one-year-old Chris Tanev is another of those young up-and-comers in the Vancouver organization that will make the team a real threat for several years to come. Yet, there is perhaps no stranger, more unpredictable success story in the NHL this year than Tanev. After all, he was never drafted, meaning all thirty NHL teams had a chance to claim him, for free, with a low draft choice—and passed. This usually means a player has to work and struggle to get a brief look-see at the NHL, but that also hasn't been the case.

Tanev played provincial junior hockey in the Toronto area and then in 2009 went to the Rochester Institute of Technology. The Tigers played in the Atlantic Conference, and this was neither a school nor a division that scouts pay great attention to. But Tanev was lucky. Vancouver's director of player development was former NHLer Dave Gagner who happened to have coached Tanev years earlier in a summer roller hockey league. Gagner watched Tanev play again in an NCAA tournament and was impressed, and signed the twenty-year-old as a free agent right after the 2009–10 season.

So in no short order Tanev went from being unwanted to leaving his NCAA program after just one year because the Canucks wanted him for their system. He became the first player from RIT to make it to the NHL.

Tanev split the past season between Manitoba and the Canucks in large part because injuries to Vancouver's blue-line necessitated call ups from the

Moose, but he also made the most of his chances. He always played double-digit minutes, and when the Moose were eliminated from the AHL playoffs he was summoned to Vancouver as insurance during the playoffs. Seeing little game action but experiencing the run to the Stanley Cup Final firsthand, he gained invaluable experience for the future.

Career Statistics	Regular Season					Playoffs				
	GP	G	A	P	Pim	GP	G	A	P	Pim
2010-11 VAN	29	0	1	1	0	for 2011 playoff stats see p. 19				

Torres, Raffi

b. Toronto, Ontario, October 8, 1981

Left wing—shoots left

6' 216 lbs.

Drafted 5th overall by NY Islanders in 2000

Another Vancouver player with roots in the Toronto area, Torres is a physical player who sometimes plays on the edge and always plays with intensity. He had an excellent junior career with Brampton in the OHL, but when he was drafted by the Islanders in 2000, he played just one more year with the Battalion before turning pro.

Torres was assigned to Bridgeport out of training camp in 2001 and over the next two years he was called up to the Islanders many times for just a game or two. In thirty-one games over two years, he didn't score a goal but he was a plus-2, indicating his checking and defensive skills. Near the trade deadline in 2003, he was sent to Edmonton with Brad Isbister for Janne Niinimaa and a second-round draft choice, and the next year he played eighty games with the Oilers.

That season saw Torres develop into an impressive player. He had 20 goals while averaging less than 13 minutes of ice time, and he was a plus-12 on a

team that missed the playoffs. The lockout forced him to find another place to play, so Torres stayed in town and spent the year with the Edmonton Road Runners, the team's new farm club. The next year, Torres was sensational, playing the best hockey of his career. He had career highs with 27 goals and 41 points and was key to getting the Oilers to the Stanley Cup Final, losing to Carolina in game seven.

The team missed the playoffs the next year, in large part because defenceman Chris Pronger left the team, and 2007–08 was marred by a serious ACL injury which forced him out of the lineup for the final fifty games of the season.

Torres was traded to Columbus in the summer of 2008 and on to Buffalo a year and a half later. Then, in the summer of 2010, he became an unrestricted free agent. Day after day passed, though, and he never got that sweet, long-term deal he was hoping for. It wasn't until some fifty-six days later that he signed a one-year, one million dollar contract in the hopes that a good season would get him exactly that career-defining offer.

In the meantime, a decent—but not spectacular—regular season paved the way for an excellent 2011 playoffs in which the bearded Torres took on all comers and played a valuable role as a two-way player.

Career Statistics	Regular Season					Playoffs				
	GP	G	A	P	Pim	GP	G	A	P	Pim
2001-02 NYI	14	0	1	1	6	DNP				
2002-03 NYI	17	0	5	5	10	DNP				
2003-04 EDM	80	20	14	34	65	DNQ				
2005-06 EDM	82	27	14	41	50	22	4	7	11	16
2006-07 EDM	82	15	19	34	88	DNQ				
2007-08 EDM	32	5	6	11	36	DNQ				
2008-09 CBJ	51	12	8	20	23	4	0	2	2	2
2009-10 CBJ	60	19	12	31	32	--	--	--	--	--
2009-10 BUF	14	0	5	5	2	4	0	2	2	12
2010-11 VAN	80	14	15	29	78	for 2011 playoff stats see p. 19				
NHL Totals	512	112	99	211	390					

Acknowledgements

The author would like to thank the many people involved in getting this book done with the utmost haste and care, starting with M & S president and publisher Doug Pepper and Jordan Fenn, publisher of the Fenn/M & S imprint, for their enthusiasm and support. Also to the editorial team at M & S, namely Liz Kribs, Michael Melgaard, Janine Laporte, and Ruta Liormonas. As well, to the designers at First Image, Michael Gray and Rob Scanlan, for taking the rough material and images and turning it into a good-lookin' book worthy of the event. To my agent Dean Cooke and his astounding assistant, Mary Hu, for sorting the business side of things out in an orderly manner. To the people at Donnelley's for a speedy turnaround from files to finished product, and to the always helpful staff at Getty, in particular Wilfred Tenaillon, Paul Michinard, Bruce Bennett, and Glenn Levy. And lastly to my personal team away from the ice— Liz, Ian, Zac, Emily, me mum, and meine frau, who just might live with me some day.

Photo Credits

All photos courtesy of Getty Images, except:
p. 98—Author's collection